Alice Fox is a textile artist who works with natural fibres and gathered materials, employing natural dyes, stitch, weave and soft basketry techniques. She studied Contemporary Surface Design & Textiles at Bradford School of Arts & Media and completed an MA in Creative Practice at Leeds Arts University. She is a member of the Textile Study Group. Alice works from her allotment and her studio, and exhibits, lectures and teaches workshops nationally and internationally.

WILD TEXTILES

WILD TEXTILES
Grown, Foraged, Found

Alice Fox

BATSFORD

First published in the United Kingdom in 2022 by
Batsford
43 Great Ormond Street
London WC1N 3HZ
An imprint of B.T. Batsford Holdings Ltd

ISBN: 9781849947879

A CIP catalogue record for this book is available from the
British Library.

30 29 28 27 26 25 24
10 9 8 7 6 5 4

Reproduction by Rival Colour Ltd, UK
Printed by Toppan Leefung Printing Ltd, China

This book can be ordered direct from the publisher at the
website: www.batsfordbooks.com.

*Some plants can present a hazard such as allergy, skin
reaction or poisoning. Use gloves and keep skin covered
when handling plants and check plant information for
toxicity warnings.*

Page 1: *Wrapped Stone:
Dandelion Braid.*
Stone, wrapped with
braided dandelion
stems and stitched
in re-purposed found
plastic.

Previous page:
(re)new threads.
A collection of 36
balls, each constructed
from hand-twisted
cordage made using
waste fabrics.

Below: Vessels made
from coiled newspaper,
re-purposed tickets,
looped cloth cordage,
eucalyptus leaf, coiled
bindweed and leaf.

Contents

Foreword

This book aims to foster a spirit of engagement with the natural world through the creative and sustainable use of textile techniques with foraged, found and grown fibres and materials. Working with the seasons and learning what materials are available at different times of year helps to ground us in natural cycles and integrates creative activity with other parts of our lives. Taking an open-minded and informed approach to resources means we can make use of what is available locally and experiment with unconventional materials.

Art enriches our lives, but it also makes us think in new ways. It can raise questions and awareness, and provide insight in a way that is approachable. If we can work in a sustainable way and help other people to think about the impact of their lives, then what we make can be a positive force for change.

Left: Coiled bindweed vessel. Dried bindweed stems coiled and stitched with bindweed.

Right: Long dandelion stems gathered for drying. These grow longest amongst tall grass.

Introduction

My previous book, *Natural Processes in Textile Art*, outlined my relationship with the natural world and how this has influenced my creative practice. I have always felt a strong desire and responsibility to live with a small environmental footprint and with consideration of the impact of my actions in all areas of life. As a global population, we are increasingly aware of the devastating impact our actions are having on the fragile planet we inhabit. We are finally understanding just how imperative it is to lessen that impact, now.

We can all make a difference in the decisions we make every day, however insignificant that may seem at times. My lifestyle is by no means perfect. While I recognize that there are always adjustments that could be made to decrease my own impact, some shifts also require changes in infrastructure that we wait for others to implement. There are, however, areas of my life – specifically my work and artistic practice – over which I have control and where I can make decisions that have a bearing on my own environmental footprint.

I took on an allotment at the same time as starting my Master's degree. The allotment plot was intended to form a focus for my practice-based research – a kind of long-term residency where I would have control over how I engaged with the site and use the materials available there. This focus would allow me to really explore the possibilities for self-sufficiency in materials for my work. I have long admired the approach that some basket-makers or woodworkers take, where all their materials are gathered or grown by themselves. The purity of the objects they produce, whether functional or decorative, is the culmination of their care and knowledge of their materials and the craftsmanship arising from working with those resources. I was seeking a way to bring that purity and honesty into my own work.

While exploring the allotment plot and the possibilities for materials that were available there, I was also exploring the ethical underpinnings of my practice. I wrote myself an artist's manifesto (shown opposite), or an expression of creative goals. This statement sums up my intentions for engagement with the materials available on my plot, but also declares my intentions for my practice in general.

Left: Gathered plant fibres drying in the allotment shed, including nettle fibre (hanging), bindweed stems, bramble stems and garlic leaves.

Below: *Hybrid Objects.* Looped cordage (bramble and sweetcorn) and random-weave bindweed with found tools, shown in the allotment shed.

My artist's manifesto:

- Develop a deep connection with place and material.

- Be as low-impact as possible.

- Use local materials as much as possible. If using new materials, make sure they are as responsibly sourced as possible.

- Be experimental. Always consider potential use of objects, materials and substance, especially before discarding anything.

- Work with natural processes. Embrace cycles of change.

- Recording activity and experience is as much an outcome as 'made' objects.

My manifesto is pinned to the studio wall and is something I come back to again and again, like a little reminder whispering in my ear whenever I am thinking about the best way to approach things and a way to stay true to the fundamentals that are important to me.

More and more artists are considering the impact of the materials they use in their work. There is increasing interest in the use of natural pigments, botanical dyes, sustainable photographic and print-making processes, natural fibres, re-purposing, and mending. With that growth in interest comes an increase in availability of information and workshops, and so the movement grows.

It is important to remember that just because a product or medium is natural, it isn't necessarily a low-impact choice. For example, plant-based pigments produced halfway around the world or cloth made from organically grown natural fibres can still have an environmental impact. Complex supply chains can make it difficult to find out exactly where and how a product has been grown, processed and finished. Being as well informed as possible about the materials you choose is one step along the way.

There is a growing number of projects worldwide that are looking to re-generate local fibre-producing systems. These are known as 'fibersheds', a model that originated in Northern California and that now has many affiliated projects (see Further Reading, page 124). Through a network of support, information sharing and connectivity, communities are increasingly able to reclaim control over how and where their fibre and textiles are produced.

Choosing to work with local, sustainable materials that you know the history of means you can work in the full knowledge of their provenance. This approach is inherently responsible. Of course, there are restrictions built into this method of working, but boundaries can also be useful in narrowing down overwhelming possibilities and pushing you to work within a set of constraints.

When you set yourself boundaries that you feel comfortable working within you also get to decide at what point to compromise. For me, this is recognizing that some basic commercially produced materials are still required, such as sketchbooks, paper, drawing pens, graphite and a few selected threads. I use new cloth in some of my workshops but also look for opportunities to re-purpose, and I encourage students to do that too. Buying less and using the materials that we already have stashed away is the most sustainable approach.

Right: Studio wall with samples, found objects and experiments.

Above: Dandelion stem
cordage in random weave.

Chapter 1

Engaging with the Natural World

Left: Bramble fibre extracted from bramble stems, hanging to dry in the allotment shed.

Localness

The fibres and processes that are included in this book are ones that I have worked with myself. My examples are specific to plants growing in the UK, so in a temperate northern climate. Whether the same plants are available or not to the reader, I explain a general approach that may be applicable to any location, and the processes will often be transferable to similar fibres in other regions.

By exploring the potential of the plants and materials that are available to me, specifically on my allotment and in my garden, my practice is rooted in my local area. By working with what I have, my environmental footprint is kept to a minimum. This approach also enables me to develop my relationship with my surroundings, appreciating what is nearby. I am constantly adding to my understanding of the materials that are at my disposal. With that growth in knowledge, I can work in a way that feels right to me. Most of these materials are humble at best or considered as weeds or waste by many. Getting to know the creative possibilities of what is often overlooked means that these materials can take on new value, as time and effort are spent on transforming them.

Connection with place

In *Natural Processes in Textile Art* and my chapter in Insights (see Further Reading, page 124), I wrote about the importance of landscape and ways of capturing a sense of place. Many of us feel deeply connected to where we live or love to visit, and feel drawn to recording that experience through our creative work:

> *Being outside or travelling through the landscape can bring a deep sense of engagement or connectedness with what I am seeing, sensing, experiencing: wonder, joy, elation, invigoration.*

I feel that my work forms a record of my experience of the natural world and that by using objects and materials that I have gathered, I am forming a tangible link to those places.

It is important that our relationship with the places from which we might gather materials is healthy and reciprocal. Understanding what makes for sensitive gathering is the key to this, so we only take a small amount of what is abundant and what we can individually make use of. Robin Wall Kimmerer explains 'the honorable harvest' (see Further Reading, page 124), which is not only based on the physical world but also in asking permission; taking only what is needed and giving thanks for it. This is the reciprocal approach that indigenous relationships form with the land. Modern society sadly often overlooks such an approach, with individual benefit winning. Kimmerer said:

Below: Dandelion stem cordage in random weave 30cm x 30cm (12in x 12in).

> *One of our responsibilities as human people is to find ways to enter into reciprocity with the more-than-human world. We can do it through gratitude, through ceremony, through land stewardship, science, art, and in everyday acts of practical reverence.*

'Commons thinking', based around shared management and harvesting with non-monetary interactions, is a particularly appropriate way of approaching resources sustainably. Traditionally, this approach related to land management, but in our digital age this can also apply to technological resources, and to communities, rituals and resources (see page 95 for more on the idea of 'commoning').

Seasonality

Once you start to understand the possibilities of the fibres and materials that are available to you locally, you will also find that there is a pattern of activity required throughout the year to make the best of opportunities for gathering. The harvesting of fibre- or plant-based dyestuffs is similar to that of grown or gathered foods. You'll learn when the best times are to harvest certain plants available to you and monitor the local conditions and those particular to each year. These patterns are not something you can learn instantly, but develop over time, along with your understanding of your local patch.

Certain times of the year bring abundance, and it can be overwhelming trying to gather everything in. It is good to recognize that if you miss the optimum gathering time one year, another will come around the next. As each growing season passes, your experience accumulates and matures. You may also find that you still have materials gathered from the previous year when the time comes for this season's harvest. Perhaps it is wise to clear out and compost any unused plant materials from the previous season once you are gathering the new crop, but this may depend on how much space you have available for storing materials.

Each person will have their own mosaic of interests and resources that develops over time related to a specific place. The pattern of seasonal activity that I have settled into for gathering and processing fibres on my plot is as follows:

Above: Processing nettle fibre with a rubber mallet for splitting open the stems; the fibre is then scraped with the back of a knife and hung to dry.

Spring: gathering and drying dandelion stems; gathering daffodil leaves (once spent). Finishing off processing fibres gathered the previous year.
Summer: gathering and stripping nettles (fresh); gathering garlic leaf, bramble fibre, bindweed, all for drying.
Autumn: drying sweetcorn husks; flax and nettle retting (see page 25) then drying.
Winter: Processing flax and nettle then spinning; constructing with all fibres.

Other materials will be gathered for dyeing, printing or constructing as and when they are available. I tend to work much more at the plot during the summer. The winter sees me working in the main studio more, processing materials and then using them in the construction of sculptural objects and surfaces.

Working with
hand-processed materials

If you are used to working with conventional or mass-produced materials, which are uniform, predictable and available in whatever amount you may require, then working with hand-gathered or processed materials can feel quite different. You may not be able to rely on the same consistency of thickness, strength or handle of a material, and quantities may be limited by what you are able to harvest and process in a season. As you work with each batch of fibre you may find that the nuances of each differ slightly from the last, tones are different, or the strands vary according to how you spun a thread or twisted some cordage. Fibres may be rougher or weaker in one year, or more robust or plentiful another year, depending on growing conditions.

If you embrace this approach, going with the flow of those differences means appreciating and really engaging with the materials, learning about their properties as you work. Along with this acceptance of challenges comes a recognition that these materials have a whole other layer of meaning and understanding attached to them. Your relationship with the work will be different, and deeper, if you have grown, harvested and handled the transformation of the raw fibre.

Many people would question why one would bother spending huge amounts of time and effort to obtain fibres when they are so readily available to buy in infinite and reliable forms. This approach is certainly not for everyone, but there is something very satisfying in producing work in this way if you are prepared to engage with the whole process. This approach is also very much about connection to the land, to the natural world and the cycles of the seasons, of growth and change and connection to your locality. Understanding the possibilities of what is around us, and engaging fully with them, underpins an appreciation for the resources, the fragility and the resilience of our environment.

Learning through the materials

Working with found, gathered and grown materials means that you will be getting to know fibres with slightly different characteristics all the time and you often have small or limited supplies of each type. It can feel like starting from scratch each time you begin to work with a new type of leaf, a particular bunch of salvaged rope or a different kind of re-purposed paper. However, as you work with different things, you will find that you slowly accumulate certain skills and intuitive responses.

I really appreciate the act of handling materials, each type or even each batch having slightly different characteristics. My hands and brain together feel their way towards a touch-based knowledge of the material. This kind of 'haptic knowledge' described by Lesley Miller (see Further Reading, page 124) is not something you can be taught – it can only come through engagement with your materials.

Inherent in the act of making is a body of knowledge formed from the intuitive decisions involved in the process. These are decisions that are not verbally pre-determined but arrived at in collaboration with the material itself.

Once you understand how to work with one particular fibre – to make cordage, for example – that understanding can be transferred onto other, similar fibres and your technique can be altered in response to the new, slightly different nature of each material you then work with.

You will also find that the characteristics of each fibre might suggest different end uses as you work with and get to know it. Some materials will dry to quite a

stiff finish, which might lend themselves to more structural applications. Others keep some flexibility or softness even when dry. These may be more appropriate for creating surfaces that require less strength or structure.

Using this book

On the following pages, I provide examples of the way I work and suggestions for other possibilities. It is not possible to give full instructions on every process or fibre that is mentioned in this book, but by giving an introduction to different fibres and materials, possibilities may be opened up that can then be researched further. A lot of the techniques and processes I use are ones I have picked up through a mixture of practical experimentation, researching in books and watching YouTube videos.

For some techniques there is really no replacement for seeing things done in person. I would recommend attending workshops with practitioners. Different people learn in different ways, but spending time in a workshop seeing an expert handling material and picking up on those nuances and practical tips for how to manage material can be very useful.

Specific instruction is given on gathering and processing some plant materials and techniques for constructing with these and other re-purposed materials. Later sections focus more on specific projects I have undertaken, outlining the steps from inspiration and investigation, illustrating how resolved pieces of work develop.

Below: Stitched and woven chestnut shells. These were worked into after the chestnut shells had dried out (see page 76).

Above: A ball of linen thread; the product of grown, gathered, hand-processed and hand-spun flax from the allotment.

Chapter 2

Grown

Left:.The allotment plot in summer with various food crops, fruit trees and flax growing (middle right).

Allotment and garden

Plant a garden. It's good for the health of the earth and it's good for the health of people. A garden is a nursery for nurturing connection, the soil for cultivation of practical reverence. And its power goes far beyond the garden gate – once you develop a relationship with a little patch of earth, it becomes a seed itself.
ROBIN WALL KIMMERER

My allotment has become the focus of my material growing and gathering, and I also collect materials from my garden. By seeing and being involved in the whole process from seed to fibre we can have a complete understanding of the resulting thread, cloth or structure. This gives us a real appreciation for the many types of cloth that surround us in our daily lives that we take for granted. Even though I am growing and producing my own linen, mine is nowhere near the fine, soft nature of the linen fabric that I like to wear, and I have huge respect for the historical production of clothing without all the technologies and global supply chains that now enable us to purchase comfort and warmth so easily.

The two main plant fibres that are grown on my plot are flax, for linen, and nettles. This chapter explains the different stages that are required in growing, harvesting and processing these two plants to make usable fibre.

Flax is sown as a crop and incorporated into the pattern of crop rotation on the allotment. Nettles grow on my plot under the fruit trees, down the side of the plot where there is hedgerow, and generally pop up in all sorts of places as they freely self-seed. I choose where to allow them to grow tall, encouraging the ones that grow in more convenient places and weeding them out from places where I don't want them. Nettles can, of course, be harvested in the wild and their ubiquitous nature means they are accessible to all.

Flax

Flax *(Linum usitatissimum)* has been grown by many cultures worldwide over thousands of years. The nature of flax's 'bast' fibres, which are long and strong, make it one of the most important fibre crops throughout history. Flax is the strongest and the most absorbent of the natural fibres. Other bast fibres include hemp, ramie, jute and milkweed. Flax fibres sit between an outer skin (cuticle) of the stem and a woody core. There are various steps of processing to remove the spinnable fibres from the other elements.

Flax is an annual plant and grows best in moist, cool conditions, making it well suited to the Northern European climate. It likes a rich soil, plenty of water and is shallow-rooted. Seeds germinate a week or so after sowing. Once the stems are around 1m (3ft) tall, small blue flowers form, lasting less than a day each and waving delicately above the graceful green stems. From sowing seed to harvesting the plants takes around 100 days and the whole plant is pulled up when the seeds have started to ripen.

Left: Flax (*Linum usitatissimum*) in flower: each delicate blue flower lasts only a few hours.

Processing flax

Once pulled up, the plants are dried off, traditionally standing in 'stooks' out in the field. I dry mine off under cover, turning the stems to dry them evenly. A series of processes then happens to extract the fibres from the stems. The seeds are removed first, either by 'rippling' (pulling the stems through a metal comb) or beating. It is important to remove these so that the oils present in the seeds don't interfere with the subsequent processes. The seeds can be saved to sow next year, used for linseed oil or used in cooking.

Retting flax

'Retting' is the next stage of processing and involves putting the stems in a damp or wet place. Retting is traditionally done in ponds or tanks (still water), in running water or laid out on grass so that the moisture of dew provides the damp conditions required. During retting, naturally occurring bacteria break down the substances holding the different stem fibres together. This allows the fibres to start to break away from the skin and the woody core of the stem. It is important to ret enough that the fibres will easily come away from the core, but not so much that the fibres are weakened.

The rate of retting will depend on air temperature and the retting conditions, so it is difficult to give an exact time for which the stems should be left retting. Monitoring the progress of the retting is important to make sure it reaches an optimum point.

I have experimented with a few different ways of retting my flax over the last few years. I have used a long deep tray, placed in the greenhouse, so the temperature was much warmer than outside. This worked but was inconvenient as the greenhouse is small. Another year I submerged my crop in an old bath at the allotment, weighing it down to keep it under water. Again, the retting was successful, and I found this batch turned much greyer, probably as a result of some iron being exposed on the surface of the bath.

I have since taken to using an old wormery that can be filled with water and has a tap at the bottom, so it is convenient to drain the water off and use it to water parts of the plot. Using these methods I find that my flax is generally retted in one to two weeks. Dew retting can take longer than this, depending on the climate and weather.

Whichever way you choose to ret your flax, it is important to keep checking progress. If a stem is broken in two and wiggled a little with the fibres coming away easily and in long strips, then the process is complete. If it has gone too far then the fibres will come away in shorter lengths. It is best to test a piece of stem that you've dried, rather than a very wet stem, as this can affect the result.

Left: 'Stooks' of dried and 'retted' flax ready for storage and then processing to remove the usable fibre.

Breaking, scutching and hackling flax

Once retted, the stems are dried off again and can then be stored in their dry state for as long as you need.

The next stages are 'breaking', 'scutching' and 'hackling'. Specific tools can be bought for these stages; if you are growing and processing a lot of flax you will need the right tools. For processing small quantities a certain amount of improvisation can be done with some basic versions.

'Breaking' involves bashing the stems to break up the core into shorter sections. 'Scutching' uses a board and a wooden tool to scrape the fibres and remove much of the core and the cuticle from amongst them. 'Hackling' involves drawing the ribbons of fibre through a set of combs called a hackle to remove the remaining fragments of core and cuticle. This results in the separation of the best and longest fibres (called 'line') and leaves behind a bundle of 'tow'; this is lower-quality fibre but can still be spun into a coarser yarn. Once the flax 'line' and tow are produced they can be spun into yarn then plied into a balanced thread.

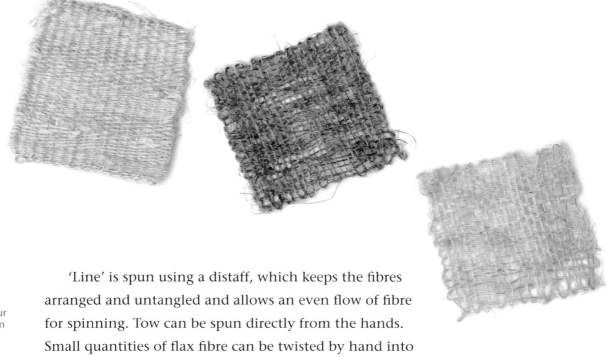

'Line' is spun using a distaff, which keeps the fibres arranged and untangled and allows an even flow of fibre for spinning. Tow can be spun directly from the hands. Small quantities of flax fibre can be twisted by hand into cordage. This is a slower process than spinning, but possibly more approachable if you're not used to spinning or only have a small quantity of fibre available.

There are many different skills included in what I have summarized here. If you want to grow and process your own, I would recommend attending a course on flax processing. This is how I first learnt about the different stages involved in taking the plant from field to loom. Various organisations, books and online resources are listed at the back of the book. There are several projects that have started up recently in the UK and further afield, researching ways of re-establishing commercial flax growing and recognizing the potential for more sustainable textiles to be produced on a variety of scales.

12
06
20

Above: Sketchbook
drawing of nettles
growing on the
allotment. Drawing
pen with home-made
botanical ink.

Nettle

Common or stinging nettles *(Urtica dioica)* grow abundantly and often near to human habitation, making them readily available for gathering. They will often colonize recently cleared ground, and grow along hedges, edges and ditches, in gardens and allotments if they're allowed, as well as in woodland and on waste ground.

Nettles have many potential uses: culinary, medicinal, and as a dyestuff. They are also a valuable plant for wildlife, with many different insects using nettles during parts of their life-cycle. Several butterfly and moth caterpillars rely on nettles as a food plant, and various insect pest controllers (ladybirds, lacewings and parasitic wasps) use nettles in their early life stages. Nettle leaves, high in nitrogen, make a good addition to compost, as mulch or to make a liquid plant food.

Fibres from nettles have been used for making textiles since pre-history and are considered to have been an important source of fibre for textiles. Knowledge about how to extract those fibres has largely been lost and overtaken by the cultivation of other fibre-rich crops. Various attempts have been made since the beginning of the 20th century to develop commercial nettle-fibre production, but none have yet been successful.

Fibre from nettle stems is often considered similar to that of flax. However, one significant difference between nettles and flax is that nettles have nodes along the stem, which make the extraction of the long, strong fibres less straightforward. Nettles also have a bark or skin that clings to the fibres, even after retting. The removal of this layer, in order to get soft fibres, adds another set of steps to go through in the processing.

There are several academics, archaeologists, artists and hobbyists researching and re-discovering how to use these freely available fibres. Allan Brown is one of these nettle enthusiasts, and has amassed a huge amount of knowledge through practical research (see page 36 for more about Allan's work). He has been instrumental in setting up the Nettles for Textiles website, a thriving online forum for sharing information (see page 125). Allan has also produced some excellent films, showing different stages of processing, which are available online. The various steps outlined below are discussed in more detail on the Nettles for Textiles website.

There are variations on approaches to processing nettle fibre, and each person who has written about their process describes the way they have found that works best for them. This may well develop and shift over time as alternative possibilities are tried. Therefore, there isn't necessarily one 'right' way to do things, but by researching different approaches, understanding some basic principles, and trying things out, you can find what works for you.

The way that nettles are processed can result in a range of different qualities of fibre, from coarse cordage to fine, soft spun thread. Obtaining usable fibre is a drawn-out process with a number of stages. If you are interested enough to put in the time and effort you will be rewarded with a truly wild fibre.

Right: A bundle of freshly cut nettle stems. The leaves have been rubbed off wearing thick gloves and the stems are ready for the fibres to be extracted and processed for drying.

Gathering nettle

In terms of fibre quality there doesn't appear to be much difference between those harvested earlier or later in the season. The best stems for harvesting are ones growing tall and that haven't been cut or disturbed during their growing season, which might result in branched stems. Nettles are valuable for a whole host of wildlife, so I feel it is best to harvest them later in the summer season, after they have set seed.

As with all foraging best practice, only take small amounts where the plant is abundant and take only what you can process. Wear long sleeves and strong gloves to minimize stings. Cut the longest stems with secateurs near to the bottom of the stem but leaving the roots of the plant intact. Holding the top of the stem, run gloved hands down the stem, stripping off the leaves and rubbing the stinging hairs from the stem. Repeat this in both directions along each stem a few times. Those stems will now have largely lost their capacity to sting and once they've dried out a bit, they will be benign.

Extracting fresh fibre from nettle

To extract fibre from fresh stems, crush the stem slightly with a stone or wooden mallet. Split the stem open from the bottom, working your way up the stem and flattening it out along its length. Holding the opened stem between nodes, crack the woody stem and start to peel away the green outer fibre from the core (which can be composted). Peel this away in both directions, approaching each node from opposite sides. Ease the fibre away from the nodes to try to maintain long continuous ribbons. These ribbons still have lots of plant pectin present, as well as the outer bark.

This fibre can be hung to dry (for a few hours or overnight) and then dampened and twisted into cordage when you are ready. Because of the gluey pectin, the resulting string will be stiff but is strong and is a fairly quick way of achieving a cord that could be used in a variety of ways.

Refining by scraping

If you want to achieve a more refined fibre with potential for spinning, you can scrape the fresh fibres to remove the bark and some of the pectin using a blunt knife. The more care you take to scrape away the fleshy parts of the ribbon, the more refined a bundle of fibres you will have. This takes time but is a way of getting good fibre without going through the retting process. This scraping needs to be done while the stems are fresh, so only pick what you can process there and then. Some pectin will still be present, even after scraping, but this will help the fibre to form a good stable yarn when dampened for either cordage or spinning.

Right: Processing nettle fibre. The fresh fibre has been split away from the woody core and is being scraped using a blunt knife to remove the bark and pectins.

Retting nettle

Nettle stems can be retted, just as you would with flax. This allows the breakdown of the gum and pectin that holds the fibres and core together. This is most easily done by laying the cut stems out on grass for 'dew retting' for a period of time (up to a few weeks, depending on temperature and weather). I dry the stems fully before laying them out. Turning the stems daily enables even retting. It is important not to over-ret, resulting in the fibres breaking down too much. The stems can be checked regularly to test whether the fibre peels away from the stem evenly. Once they are sufficiently retted, the stems should be gathered in and dried for storage.

To extract the fibre from the stems, flatten each stem in turn using a stone, wood or by standing on them so that they start to split open. Prise open the stem along its length then snap the woody core between nodes, peeling the strips of bast fibre towards each node. Easing the fibres off at the nodes takes some care, and it can be difficult to take the whole ribbon of fibre from a stem without it breaking at the nodes.

Right: Nettle fibre extracted from the stems and processed fresh, then allowed to dry before use.

Processing and carding nettle

Once the ribbons of fibre are extracted from the woody parts (which can be composted or used for paper-making), the fibre can go through another process of rolling and scraping to remove the bark and result in softer fibre. Sections of the fibre can be rolled vigorously between the hands or against your thigh, which will start to rub off some of the bark. This is best done outside as it creates fine dust. This process starts to soften the fibres. They can then be scraped with a blunt knife to remove even more of the bark. The more work that is put into these processing stages, the softer the fibre will be, but also more of the fibre is lost along the way as 'tow'. The long fibres can be combed or hackled (as in flax processing). Any of the tow fibres that come away during this activity can be carded (using wool carders) and then spun.

Some practitioners may choose not to go through the rolling and scraping stages but take the stripped fibre directly to carding. This will remove some of the bark and will provide a woolly fibre suitable for spinning but will produce a coarser yarn than that having been rolled and scraped as well.

Field or root retting

This method is written about by Birte Ford (see Further Reading, page 124). Ford allows the nettles to stay outside, uncut, during the winter, so that the breaking down of the pectin and so on is done by the weather over a longer period of time. Ford then bakes the gathered and dried stems before splitting the fibre from the woody stem (the boon). This method works for the climate and conditions of Scotland, where Ford lives and works. Having gathered some over-wintered nettles on my own patch, I have found that generally the fibres are too weak to be able to reliably use this method.

Above: Nettle cordage made using fibre stripped from fresh stems and processed by scraping. The bright green of the fresh fibre mellows with time to rich golden brown.

Left: Nettle yarn spun from fibre that was extracted from retted stems, splitting the fibre from the core and then carded before spinning.

Allan Brown

Allan Brown, who has helped set up Nettles for Textiles, describes in his own words his discovery of nettle fibre gathering and processing, leading him to create a full garment from this humble fibre.

'My interest in using locally foraged nettle fibre to create textiles arose naturally from a period when I was tramping through the Sussex countryside with a wild-flower identification book, learning what was edible, medicinal or useful for cordage and fire-making. It soon became apparent that nettles were the most abundant and reliable source of fibre, as well as food. I began to ponder whether it was possible to create a wearable textile from them, and, if this indeed was the case, then where and when had this been done before? I had no previous experience in any form of textile creation and, beyond fairy tales, there were very few sources at the time describing in detail how one would go about turning nettles into cloth. I just began to experiment and started to develop the skills I would need to realize this dream.

I looked into how the other bast-fibre plants such as flax and hemp were processed and tried to apply those methods to nettles. I started to grow flax on my allotment and this soon extended to growing dye plants with which to colour the rough yarns I was creating. As well as being enamoured by the idea of creating clothing from my local surroundings, I wanted to do so in the most environmentally sensitive way possible. I hoped to demonstrate that even living in an urban environment, using readily available resources like allotments, parks and gardens, that it was possible to feed and clothe oneself without needing to own land.

Once I began to produce small woven samples of nettle cloth and gained confidence that it was indeed possible, I decided that I would make a nettle dress, to reflect the fairy-tale nature of the whole endeavour. It took me several years and thousands of nettles to spin up enough yarn with which to weave the cloth. In order to ensure that the yarn would take the tension of a floor loom, the warp was a ply of nettle and allotment-grown line fibre flax, while the weft was a pure nettle single. Once off the loom, the woven cloth, which up until this point had required no additional inputs like heat, chemicals or water, was scoured in wood ash and 'beetled' or softened by pressing the cloth between a heavy stone from the beach and a wooden board.

The pattern for the dress was based on medieval 'cotes', a simple but enduring design that utilizes the woven selvedges with little or no wastage from cutting the cloth into the various pattern pieces. The dress will be stitched together with a hand-spun nettle and flax thread.'

Above: 'Beetling' or softening the woven nettle cloth, with a smooth beach stone. This involves pressing, as opposed to rubbing, the cloth in order to soften the fibres and transform the fabric from a stiff surface to a cloth with drape.

Right: Weaving the cloth: Nettle and flax warp on the loom with pure nettle weft on the shuttle.

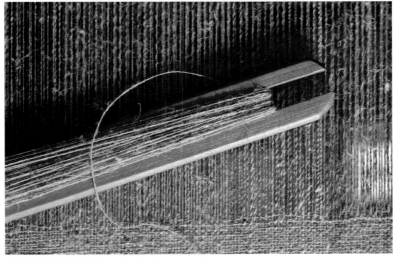

Above: *Pear Leaf Quilt* (detail).
Leaves with hand stitch in plant
dyed cotton/silk thread.
30 x 30cm (12 x 12in)

Chapter **3**

Foraged

Working with weeds

Plants become weeds when they obstruct our plans, or our tidy maps of the world. If you have no such plans or maps, they can appear as innocents, without stigma or blame.
RICHARD MABEY

'Weed' is a negative term for a plant growing in what we consider the wrong place. As Richard Mabey explains: *with weeds context is everything* (see Further Reading, page 124). He goes on to point out that: *Weeds made the first vegetables, the first home medicines, the first dyes.*

I feel that 'wild plants' is a more positive label for these common self-seeders, which are often growing where they can take advantage of conditions that we've created through our own activity. I am trying to use things that are classed as weeds just as much as I might use the things I plant – there are possibilities with weeds just as for cultivated plants. Wild plants are the key to biodiversity, providing food for invertebrates and all the rest of the food chain beyond.

My garden and allotment are a slightly riotous mix of cultivated plants, sown or planted specifically, and self-seeded plants, which I can choose whether to leave in place or 'weed' out. This is an ongoing conversation between gardener and plants. In turn, this mix of cultivated and wild allows for a variety of insect life, pollinators and predators all doing their thing as part of the natural life cycle.

I've really enjoyed getting to know some of the less obvious materials available on my allotment – dandelions, for instance, which have lovely shiny stems when used in soft basketry techniques. This successful and tenacious plant can be a

Above: Woven bindweed vessel. Random weave with dried bindweed stems.

Left: Sketchbook drawing of whole dandelion (*Taraxacum officinale*) plant. Drawing pen with home-made botanical inks.

source of annoyance for gardeners, but I have learnt to appreciate it as a valuable asset for wildlife and as a source of materials. It is also edible and there are a host of traditional tales and folklore attached to it. Bindweed *(Calystegia sepium)* is another plant that gardeners tend to dislike and will take over if you don't keep on top of its rapid growth but I know I can gather, dry and make use of the stems.

I'm more of an opportunistic forager than a strategic one. I tend to gather things that I know I can use when I find them rather than going looking, although there are some materials that I know I can collect on local walks at certain times of year. Most of my materials come from my plot, but these are supplemented by others foraged elsewhere. Responsible gathering was discussed earlier (see page 15) and is something that should underpin any foraging activity.

Leaf stitching

I wrote about leaf stitching in *Natural Processes in Textile Art*. Since writing that book, I have continued to work with gathered fallen leaves in a variety of ways. When I first started exploring leaf stitching, trying out different leaves that were available to me locally became really absorbing and led to a whole body of work based around the simple idea of stitching leaves together.

I see leaf stitching as a good way to understand the potential of natural materials – I enjoy the process of getting to know a material by working with it. As discussed earlier, it is only by handling and manipulating a material that you can start to understand the nuances of its possibilities and limitations. Collecting a series of different leaf types on a walk and then experimenting with them will lead you to a new set of practical knowledge.

You can ask yourself:

- Which leaves are easier to work with?
- Which leaves tear more easily than others?
- How can you hold the leaves as you stitch so that they are less likely to tear or crumble?
- Which varieties are better to work with fresh and which will be easier to work with when they've been dried?
- Which type of needle and thread are easiest to work with?

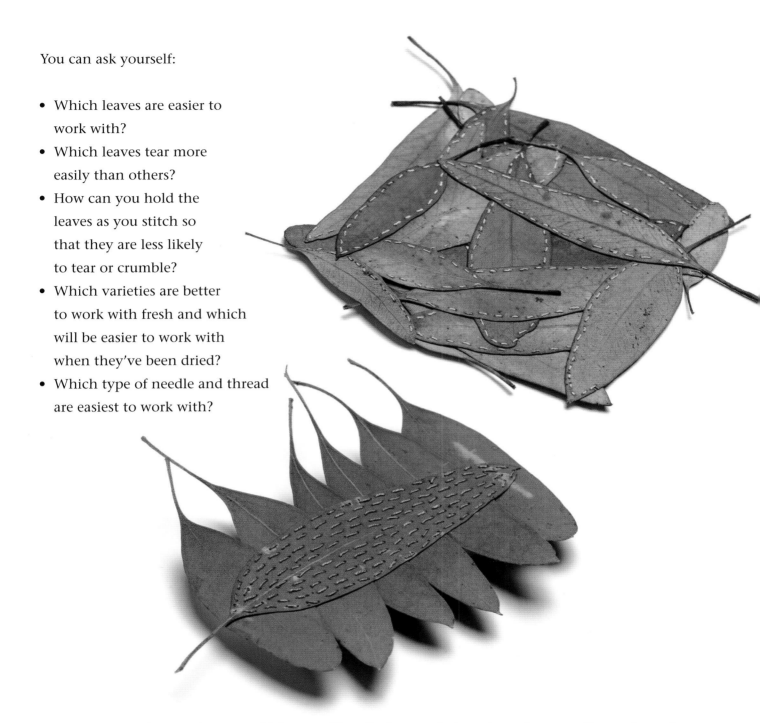

It is only by trying this out for yourself that you'll really know what works and what doesn't. I started off stitching leaves onto a paper background, which supported the leaves as I stitched. As I became more confident in handling the leaves, I found ways to stitch them together without any additional support. I find a sharp fine needle makes a real difference.

The eucalyptus tree at the bottom of my street drops leaves frequently. These are lovely to work with when they are fresh, being strong and flexible, and releasing a lovely aroma as you stitch. As they dry, they become more brittle and therefore less satisfactory to work with.

Above and opposite: Stitched eucalyptus leaves: a series of experiments stitching, patching, and joining eucalyptus leaves with hand stitch in plant-dyed silk/cotton thread.

Other leaves, such as many of the broad-leaved tree species, are less robust when fresh and tear easily. I find that these can benefit from drying for a week or so, pressed between paper and under the weight of a couple of books.

Once you've learnt which leaf types or species are most satisfying to work with, you can extend the different ways you might use them. Patching and joining leaves in different combinations can result in some interesting surfaces. If you work with fresh (or partly dried) leaves then they will need a period of drying after your construction is complete. For flat pieces this means pressing them between

paper and under the weight of a few books. Once they are fully dried, they should stay flat. You may prefer to let the stitched leaves to dry without pressing, allowing them to curl and take on whatever sculptural form they find for themselves.

I am often asked about whether the stitched leaves will disintegrate. They will certainly become brittle as they dry, and the colours will fade slowly. Fading will happen quicker if they are exposed to bright daylight. But if they are kept dry and protected (for instance, if they are mounted in a frame) then they have the potential to stay as they are for many years.

Above: *Eucalyptus Quilt.* Leaves with hand stitch in plant-dyed cotton/ silk thread. 40 x 20cm (16 x 8in).

Left: *Oak Leaf Quilt* (detail). Leaves with hand stitch in plant-dyed cotton/silk thread. 50 x 50cm (19¾ x 19¾ in).

Below: *Apple Leaf Quilt.* Leaves with hand stitch in plant-dyed cotton/silk thread. 17 x 17cm (16¾ x 16¾in).

Right: *Pear Leaf Quilt.* Leaves with hand stitch in plant-dyed cotton/silk thread. 30 x 30cm (12 x 12in).

Leaf quilts

I love the way that leaves fall on the ground in the autumn, making their own kind of organic patchwork. I wanted to explore this idea of a patchwork quilt made with the leaves themselves. Stitching round the edges of individual leaves and taking advantage of the overlapping and layering to support the surrounding leaves as I stitched, I built up a sheet of stitched leaves without any other supporting material. Using the same technique with different types of leaves, I found that slight differences in the thickness and the fragility of the different species really affected the potential for building up the quilt.

Having made *Oak Leaf Quilt* with leaves from a local wood, I wanted to try leaves from my allotment fruit trees. The leaves from the pear tree (opposite) and the apple tree (right) seemed very similar, but when it came to stitching them, the apple leaves were that bit harder to work with, so resulted in a smaller quilt. This is another example of learning the nuances of the particular material through practical research, the results of which I couldn't have predicted.

Leaf vessels

There are many traditions around the world for using leaves in practical ways to make vessels or containers. Often very simple in construction, these structures are born out of necessity and of indigenous knowledge of local materials. These might take the form of platters, bowls, vessels or wrapped packaging.

Exploring the possibilities of forming vessel structures with leaves available to you locally is another way to engage with these less-conventional materials, finding ways to join, manipulate and form the leaves.

It can be useful to use another object to help form the leaves into the shape you want, either to stitch around or to keep the leaves in the

Above and right:
Leaf Cubes. Leaves formed around a wool felt cube and hand stitched before drying.

Left: Leaf vessel sample. Leaves layered and hand stitched to make a vessel form before drying.

desired form while they dry. I made a series of leaf cubes, each one formed by folding a large leaf around a felt cube that I had constructed beforehand, and that stayed inside the folded and stitched leaf.

When forming stitched-leaf vessels, I find it helpful to sit the vessel inside a bowl of the required depth so that it is supported underneath, then I use scrunched paper to keep the leaves from curling as they dry. Once the leaves have fully dried, they will keep their shape, but will also become more brittle and should be handled with care as they will easily break if knocked.

Above: *Eucalyptus Leaf Vessel.* Leaves arranged tonally and joined with hand stitch to make a shallow vessel form before drying. 20 x 20 x 5cm (8 x 8 x 2in).

Hillary Waters Fayle

Hillary Waters Fayle combines embroidery with botanical material. Here she describes why she works with leaves.

'I bring together materials and processes that express the union of humanity and the physical world, most often textile traditions in collaboration with botanical material. The deep historical and lived experience we have with cloth echoes our connection to the botany all around us: both are entwined with our evolution and survival, and they are so integrated into our lives that they become nearly invisible.

Plants are our food, our fuel, they are the base of our food chains, supporting all forms of life on the planet. Leaves are infinitely replenishable, uniquely exquisite, ubiquitous to the point of being taken for granted. Plants connect us directly to the land, grounding us in our understanding of our place on the planet. Through botany we see reflections of our own lives: the magic and excitement of new energy sprouting forth, blooming and fullness of maturity, the withering of beauty and the eventuality of death. We are reminded that to all winters, there are summers; for all that goes dormant there is a resurgence of growth. Plants teach us of the importance of strong roots, and that magnificent things can come from tiny seeds. We can take lessons about patience and gratitude from the flora around us, for if there is soil and water and if the sun still shines, that is enough.

Whether stitching, drawing, planting seeds, or harvesting, my hands echo the gestures made by thousands of hands over thousands of years and I feel connected to the lineage of people working with textiles, plants and the land. Stitching, like horticulture, can be functional or it can be done purely in service of the soul, lifting the spirit through beauty and wonder.

Although an uncommon surface to stitch on, leaves almost always prove to be stronger than they appear. Organic materials can be challenging to work with and require preservation and especially gentle handling, but there is a sense of magic in being able to work with such an unexpected and exquisite material. The tension in the thread, the type of stitching, the needle, the species, and the season are just some of the factors that may influence what happens. There is always a conversation happening between my hands and the leaves through the thread; it feels collaborative and rewarding to work with material that requires such sensitivity and attention.'

Above: *Weight of Worth* (2017). Ginkgo leaf and thread. 13 x 18cm (5 x 7in).

Left: *Patterns of Transcendence* (2021). Magnolia leaf and thread. 26 x 10cm (10¼ x 4in).

Kitchen foraging

Realising the potential of leaf material, seed cases and other such organic items as surfaces for stitching can open other possibilities to you for unconventional materials to work with.

Teaching a workshop a few years ago in southern Ireland, my host, Joan Mulvany, had made a beautiful bowl of stitched avocado skins, and I started stitching into some myself when I returned home. Stitched when fresh, the skins are pliable and easy to pierce. They then dry, shrinking a little, to form hard little vessels. Joan explains her approach:

Sometimes when I look at things I think 'what can I do with this?', and the beautiful avocado is no exception. In a small attempt to justify its journey from where it was grown to its destination in our kitchen, I collect the skins and stones for dyeing. I usually leave the skins on the windowsill to dry and they become quite shrivelled. Word travelled, and pals began to donate their avocado skins to me. I started looking at them and decided the next avocado skin was going to be stuffed with tissue to try and keep its shape. Now, I was paying it attention and the next day I checked it out, and it was keeping a lovely open shape, AND it also had the feel of soft leather. This was the time I decided I could try and stitch into it. The skin is lovely to stitch into. I have also dried pomegranate skins, trying to keep a concave shape to the skin when I am drying it, and catching it when it is pliable enough to stitch. Again, these are a treat to stitch into.

Above and below: A series of avocado skins, hand stitched when fresh and allowed to dry, sometimes distorting the stitches.

Left: Dried avocado skins, one with hand stitch, gathered by Joan Mulvany.

Cordage

Above: Cordage
samples using a variety
of materials from
the allotment plot,
including plant stems,
leaves, found cloth,
paper and plastic.

Archaeologists have found evidence of string-making from between 20,000 and
30,000 years ago. It is recognized that the making of spun or twisted threads was
a necessary development that allowed things to be tied, bound and carried, and for
woven cloth to be made. This very basic but fundamental method of manipulating
fibres opens up a whole range of possibilities for constructing and joining.

Cordage or string-making involves the addition of twist to fibre to make a
thread that is generally much stronger than the individual fibres. Adding twist
in two opposing directions creates a 'Z-S' twist, which won't unravel.

There will need to be joins between units of fibre; the frequency of these
will depend on what the fibres are. For instance, a daffodil or iris leaf may be
30cm (12in) or more, whereas a piece of sweetcorn husk will be more like
10–15cm (4–6in). Joins in the two twisted elements should be stepped, so that
your string can be as even as possible. Most leaves or stems will vary in thickness
from base to tip, so care should be taken to keep the string as even as possible, by
adding new fibres in before the existing cordage gets too thin or cutting off thicker
sections at the base before adding in.

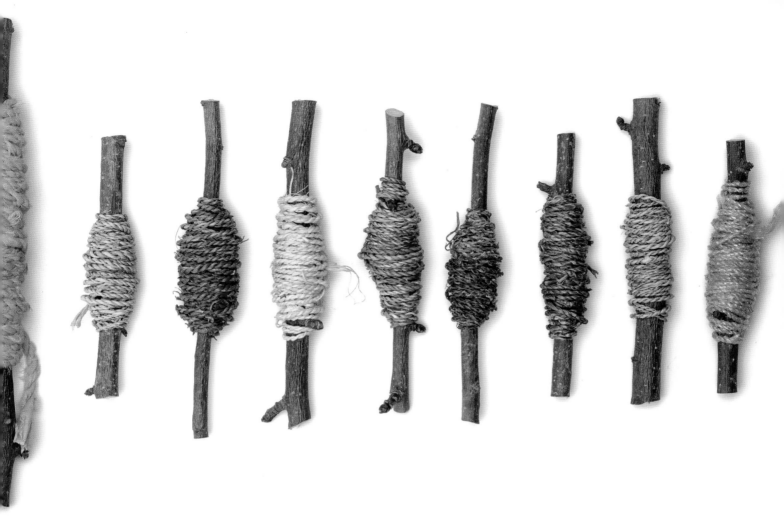

There are different techniques for making the twist and forming cordage. A look through some online videos will show you a variety of approaches appropriate for diverse materials. Some techniques are just personal preference. I have tried various ways of making cordage and find that I prefer to add the twist by rolling between the fingers of my left hand while holding the developing string in my right. I roll the fibre of the furthest strand (top in diagram) away from me between my fingers and then bring that strand across the other one and towards me, thus twisting them against each other. I am not left-handed but seem to have ended up with a left-handed approach becoming my established and intuitive way. I make cordage largely by feel once I am in the rhythm of working with a particular material.

Roll away

Twist across front

Roll away

Twist across front

Gathering, drying, storing and managing plant-based materials

When working with plant fibres to make cordage or to manipulate stems or leaves into constructed surfaces and structures, the general rule is to gather materials and dry them out before use. This allows the fibres to lose their water content and therefore do any shrinking at this point. The materials can then be stored indefinitely until you are ready to use them.

It is important to store materials in dry conditions and without being wrapped in plastic so as to avoid mould developing. I have learnt the hard way how easily a season's crop of a particular material can be lost when left too long in a slightly damp place. Storing materials in cloth or paper bags is convenient and won't allow condensation that might form with plastic bags. Alternatively, bunches of materials can be tied and hung from strings or hooks, allowing air flow around them.

Once you are ready to work with the plant material, dampen it with water using a spray bottle and wrap it in

Above: Gathering spent daffodil leaves. These should only be gathered once they have started to die back naturally.

a damp cloth for an hour or so to 'mellow'. This will soften the fibres and allow them to change from their dry, brittle state to a flexible and surprisingly strong condition that you can manipulate through your chosen technique.

Allowing the fibres to shrink through that early drying avoids them shrinking when they are part of a structure and resulting in loosening of your careful work. This harvesting, drying then re-dampening process applies to materials such as daffodil, iris and similar long strap-like leaves or dandelion stems. Some plant materials can be worked with while fresh, but it is important to be aware that they will shrink as they dry out and to allow for that as you work with them.

Other plant materials will require some processing when fresh to remove and separate the usable fibre from other parts of the stem or leaf, so that you can then dry them out and store until ready to use. This applies to fibres such as those from bramble, willowherb or hollyhock stems. The stems are scraped of their outer bark-like skin (and thorns, in the case of brambles), split, then the strong fibres

Above: Processing bramble fibre. A blunt knife is used to scrape the bark away, in this case before extracting the fibre from the woody core.

are peeled from the woody inner stem and dried. These then need to be dampened to work with them.

The leaves of some more robust plants, like members of the cordyline family that are often used as architectural garden plants, can be used with a variety of approaches to obtain useable fibre. These leaves can be divided into sections, dried and then used as flat strips, or they can be left to 'field ret' over some weeks of winter, during which time they will start to break down and separate out into fibres. These can be combed to separate the fibres further and then used for cordage or coiling. The fresh leaves can also be scraped to remove the fleshy part and reveal the fibres within.

Processing of plant fibres to take them from harvest to useable material can be time-consuming and repetitive. These materials are hard-won, but the slow progress and hard work can be outweighed by the meaning that is imbued by that personal hand processing. Nurturing something from seed to harvest and then onwards to art materials increases the personal value and ties the resulting artwork to the land and conditions that provided the plants. This isn't for everyone – it is certainly quicker and easier to buy commercially produced materials – but for those who are seeking a deeper connection with where their materials come from and with the landscape that produced them, there are many ways to engage on this more involved level.

Harvesting each fibre will be best at certain times of the year, so fibres should be gathered when they are abundant and ready and then dried and stored for use later in the year. Just as we would harvest food plants when ripe and abundant, storing things away for the leaner times of year, we can take the same approach to plant fibres.

Useful plants

Some examples of plants commonly found in gardens or vegetable plots that can be harvested for fibre:

Daffodil (*Narcissus*): after flowering, allow the leaves to start to die back. This allows the plant's energy to go back into the bulb to be stored for next year. Once the leaves are yellow or brown they can be gathered and dried.

Iris (*Iris*) and day lily (*Hemerocallis*): any of these types of plant with long strappy leaves can be made use of. Either harvest leaves after flowering when still green or wait for the plants to die back later in the year and gather the leaves when brown.

Dandelion stems (*Taraxacum officinale*): once the flowers are over and ideally after seeds have dispersed (the flowers and seeds are valuable to a host of wildlife), pick the longest stems and allow them to dry. Look for particularly tall stems that are growing amongst long grass rather than the small ones that come up through cracks in paving or are regularly mowed.

Bramble (*Rubus fruticosus*): look for long green stems during summer that are formed from that year's growth and that don't have branches coming off them. Wear thick gloves. Cut with secateurs as close to their base as possible. Run a gloved hand along the stem, rubbing off the thorns and leaves. The fibre should then be scraped with a blunt knife to take away the waxy outer skin. The stems can then be bashed along their length with a mallet or stone and the fibre peeled away from the woody core. The fibre can then be dried.

Raspberry (*Rubus idaeus*): raspberry canes can be split down and stripped in a similar way to bramble, removing the fibre that sits between the outer skin and the woody core.

Sweetcorn (*Zea mays*): the outer husks from corn-on-the-cob can be peeled off when the corn is ripe and ready to eat. Allow the husks to dry and then they can be stripped down ready for use. I strip these down while still dry using a sharp metal comb (I use one from a pet-supplies shop) and then dampen those strips for use. If you have enough of them, the silky tassels from the top of the cob can also be collected, dried and then used for cordage.

Rhubarb (*Rheum rhabarbarum*): peel off the outer fibres from the stem using a sharp knife, separate out the fibrous strips and dry. These give off a wonderful aroma when handled to make cordage.

Horseradish (*Armoracia rusticana*): the leaves of this vigorous plant have fibrous stems, which can be split down and scraped using a blunt knife to reveal strong, silky strands.

Soft rush (*Juncus effusus*): this common rush grows abundantly in rough, damp, grassy areas and bog edges. The stems can be harvested when they are at their longest, pulling from the base of the plant. They can be dried and then dampened to use for braiding, twining and other soft basketry techniques. The fresh stems can also be combed and beaten with a wooden mallet in bundles, stripping the stems down and removing the inner spongy core. This fibre is dried and then dampened for use in cordage-making.

Some house plants can provide string-making material. Many people have spider plants *(Chlorophytum comosum)* as easy-care houseplants. The leaves periodically dry and wither. If those browning leaves are collected and dried until enough are collected to work with, they make an excellent and surprisingly strong cordage.

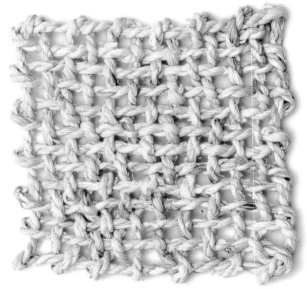

Woven samples, each
5 x 5cm (2 x 2in).

Top: Nettle fibre
cordage, spun flax
(linen) and spun
flax (linen).

Centre: Sweetcorn
husk cordage,
newspaper cordage
and cabbage palm
(*Cordyline australis*)
cordage.

Bottom: dandelion-
stem cordage, spun
flax (linen) tapestry
weave and spun
nettle fibre.
·

Braiding dandelions

The technique for making cordage by twisting two strands together, as described on page 55, can be extended into braiding with different numbers of strands. The samples here show how dried dandelion stems can be manipulated into different widths of braid, which have possibilities for joining together and therefore creating wider surfaces or three-dimensional structures.

Right: Dandelion stems mellow during drying from light green to golden yellows and browns.

Far right: Plaiting or braiding the stems using three and five stems.

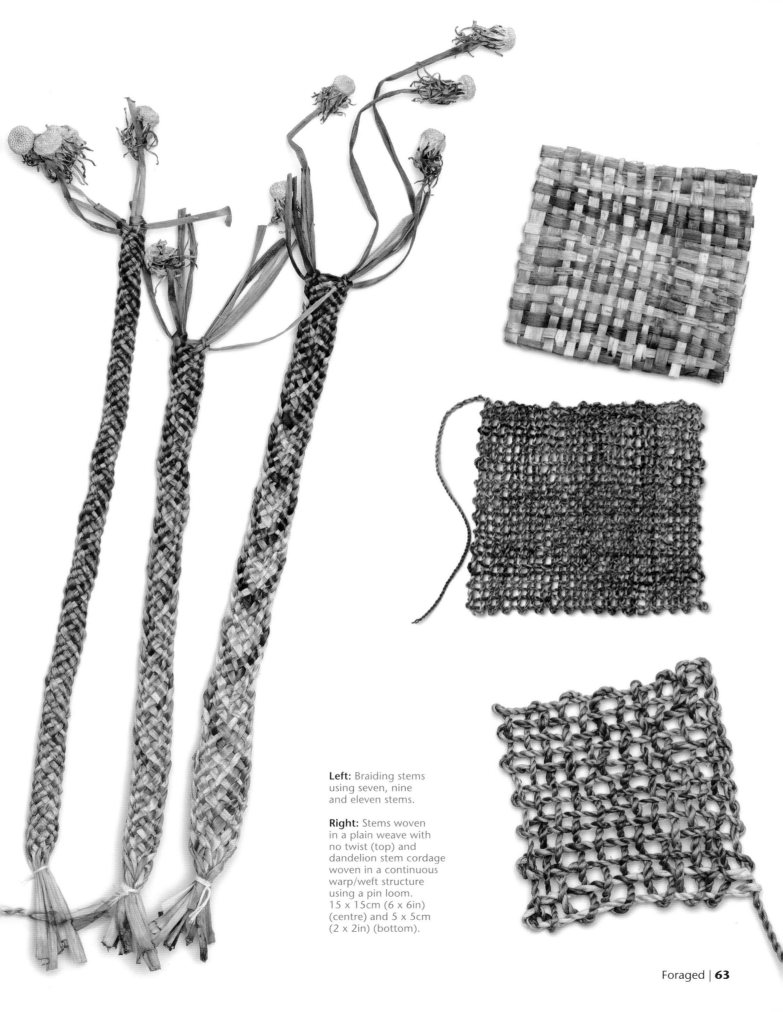

Left: Braiding stems using seven, nine and eleven stems.

Right: Stems woven in a plain weave with no twist (top) and dandelion stem cordage woven in a continuous warp/weft structure using a pin loom. 15 x 15cm (6 x 6in) (centre) and 5 x 5cm (2 x 2in) (bottom).

Foraged | **63**

Penny Maltby

An artist in multiple mediums, here Penny Maltby describes why she was drawn to work with straw.

'Thinking through making and experimentation is at the core of my practice and has given me a passion for the history and narrative behind traditional heritage crafts and cultural heritage. This tacit knowledge and cultural heritage was once passed on from generation to generation, but many of the relevant skills in heritage crafts are very time-consuming to learn, poorly perceived and undervalued, resulting in them becoming endangered or extinct. There are also challenges in obtaining specialist materials and tools. I am interested in using traditional crafts in new ways and settings. I am seeking possibilities by using the past to help shape new ideas and hope to make them relevant and engaging to new generations.

Left: Studio wall samples and experiments, assorted sizes 10–60cm (4–24in). Circular tied straw work with experimental embroidery; red cotton and straw on calico, spiral plait; Maris Widgeon straw and cotton thread, waffle weave sample; linen warp with linen and straw splint weft.

Below: Detail from large straw sculpture (2021). Straw marquetry. Rye and wheat straw, five-straw spiral plait, seven-straw hat plait.

Straw (which covers wheat, rye and oat) is a wonderful discovery for me, both in its material properties and its significance to our agricultural, industrial and cultural history. It is ever present in our landscape, in thatched roofs and fodder and bedding for animals. This humble material is versatile to work with; used whole, it gives structure and can be plaited into hollow forms such as corn dollies and braid forms with intricate patterns and designs. It can be split and flattened for fine work like weaving and embroidery, and it can be spun into thread. The colours can vary from greens to rich golden yellow. It can be dyed, shredded, and pulped and used to make paper and fabric.

Specialist growers of heritage wheat varieties needed for different types of straw work are limited. It is a lower-yield crop than modern varieties, requires different harvesting and drying techniques and is more prone to adverse weather. I source mine from a farm in Staffordshire where the farmer grows Maris Widgeon and rye varieties especially for straw work. She is continuing a decades-old tradition started by her father. The straw needed must be one of the old varieties with a nice long hollow stem; most work uses the first part from the base of the ear down to the first node. Good preparation is key, but is also labour-intensive and repetitive.

As a maker I can see and feel the differences in the harvest from year to year, with changes in length, colour and texture. Fortunately, it stores well, so I buy extra when it is a good year. Recently there has been more interest in heritage grains for bread-making and baking, which may help to encourage more growers to use traditional methods and varieties; this is great news for thatchers and straw craftspeople alike.'

Suburban foraging

In autumn and winter, suburban pavements and country lanes are littered with fallen leaves and twigs blown down from trees in high winds. As these bits of debris are repeatedly walked over, driven over and exposed to rain and cold, the fibres are slowly broken down. If you look closely, you may find stems or branches that are separating out into fibres that could be used to make cordage. The processing of some plant fibres in order to extract usable fibre can involve repeated beating or combing. For these windfalls, it is almost like they have been beaten and, as a result, their outer layers have gone and their inner long

Above: Weathered and partially broken-down leaf stems on a suburban street.

Right: Cordage made from leaf stems that have been gathered from suburban streets during the winter after a period of weathering.

Above: Cordage and woven cordage samples made from weathered cabbage palm (*Cordyline australis*) fibre gathered from suburban streets.

Left: Cordyline vessel in random weave using weathered cabbage palm fibre. 15 x 15 x 7cm (6 x 6 x 2¾in)

fibres are exposed. Gathering these fibres up, they can be dampened, just like any other dried plant material, and twisted into a rough string.

In some areas, where cordyline species grow well (for example, in southern coastal areas here in the UK), the old leaves of these species often fall and ret naturally. I have gathered bundles that have fallen from gardens onto pavements and roads, been walked and driven over by passing pedestrians and traffic while damp from rain and, as a result, are in a good state to use for cordage.

Above: Coiled bindweed
vessel (detail). Dried bindweed
stems coiled and stitched
with bindweed.

Chapter 4

Found

Foraged from nature

Basket weaver Lois Walpole beautifully describes her transition from using bought materials for her baskets to using only materials that are gathered or found, including cardboard, juice cartons and plastics (see Further Reading, page 124). She outlines the benefits she found in limiting herself to using only found materials:

> *These I gathered from the streets around my home ... or from the weekly food shopping. In so doing I discovered that they had lots of advantages over bought materials ... Using materials that were considered to be of no value would speak far more clearly and with more force about what I saw as an appalling waste of resources than anything I could actually say about it.*

Sometimes when we give ourselves a set of constraints to work within it can really push us to be more creative and focused, just as I found when I embarked on my allotment-based project and as I described in the introduction to this book.

Some found materials can easily be used to replace those that we might have bought and be applicable to some of the techniques that have been mentioned already. But foraging can also result in collecting groups of natural objects, collected purely for their beauty and interest rather than for obvious use as a material for textile-related activity.

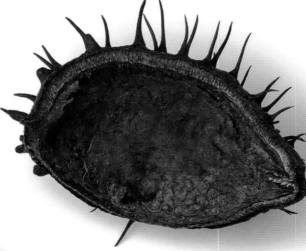

Natural objects such as seashells, pebbles, and seeds and their cases are a constant source of interest and wonder on a small scale. Finding ways to engage with these objects creatively can add another layer of appreciation and knowledge about their properties and materiality.

Some of these items can be stitched through or drilled in order to pass a needle and thread through them. This means that they could be joined, or they could form the basis of some sort of stitched or woven structure. However, it may not be possible to drill or make holes in hard materials such as stone or metal. Such objects will

Left and above: Various found natural objects that might be used as inspiration or worked into with stitch, weave or looping techniques.

need a different approach if they are to be worked with and responded to using textiles techniques.

If it isn't possible to make holes through the material, and therefore stitch through it, then there are possibilities for wrapping or encasing the object in some sort of stitched, looped or woven structure. I have worked with a range of different natural materials in this experimental way, each time finding methods of working into or onto the forms.

Wrapping

There are various traditional cultural practices from around the world that involve wrapped rocks. One tradition that I am drawn to is the Japanese practice of *tome ishi* or 'stop stone', where rocks are bound with twine and placed on pathways as a sign that means 'no entry'. This device is used to guide people along a desired route, using understanding rather than anything more forceful.

Fundamental to practices such as this are choosing the right rock and twine, and a reciprocity of agreement between the person placing the stone and those coming across it and 'reading' the message. Other stone-wrapping traditions have developed out of meditation and contemplation practices, involving repetitive actions and producing objects that might function as amulets.

A series of wrapped stones I made as part of *Findings*, an exhibition project (above), were not made with any specific meaning attached them, but rather as a personal response to the place and to the technical challenge of working with gathered stones. Collecting a series of smooth pebbles from a coastal location in North Yorkshire, I was struck by the idea of wrapping as a way of engaging with the pebbles creatively. But wrapping a smooth stone with thread that just slips off is not as straightforward as it might seem. So, a series of experiments unfolded, through which I found a way to bind the pebbles, stitching through the layers of wrapped threads to create a stable structure held in place around each individual stone.

Once I had figured out a technique that worked, I was able to play with the density of wrapping and stitching, building up a series of pieces that reveal different amounts of the stone surface underneath. Using mud collected from the same site, rubbed on to my wrapped threads, shifts the surface again from soft fibre to another layer of stone. This collection of wrapped stones became the result of experimenting and learning about the materials I was working with, but it also holds the memory of the place from where the stones were collected, noticing the detail around me at the time and all that goes along with that experience:

On the beach, low tide. Round the headland on the exposed flats of rock. Fossils embedded and half exposed. Layers of rock on slightly different levels have different characteristics: cracks, formations, textures, colours. Slippery under foot. This place feels timeless. Water runs and drips down the cliff face. A flock of corvids dance in the air. Bright light on distant waves. Thundering noise and bitterly cold wind. Smooth dark pebbles, almost black. Iron-rich muds flow out of the cliffs, almost glowing with their orange-red hues.

Notes made on working with the stones:

Experiments in wrapping these smooth pebbles are tentative at first: there is nothing on the surface to stop my linen threads from slipping off. Perseverance finds me developing a way of wrapping and stitching as I go, slowly building up a tight structure that holds the stone. Stitching around a form: tracing the form again and again as it is turned in the hand. Constructing a form that fits around the object, like creating a portrait of the item, one becomes aware of all the nuances of the form and surface. A piece of mud-stone, when wet, rubbed on the surface of my threads marks the linen with a new layer of 'stone'.

Above: Linen-wrapped stones. Smooth pebbles wrapped and stitched with linen thread in different densities.

Left: 'Stop Stone' *tome ishi*. Stone wrapped with cordage made from soft rush (*Juncus effusus*) used as a sign not to go any further along this path.

Weaving

Another way of working with those smooth pebbles that I described when discussing wrapping (pages 72–73) was to create small bespoke woven surfaces that could fit around the pebbles themselves. By making a paper template of the shape of an individual pebble, I was able to build up a woven surface on a simple wooden frame. This could then be cut free from its tensioned warp and be manipulated into a three-dimensional form that would encase the pebble. I also made some of these to fit a stone but left the stone out after forming the woven form, so that the woven surface formed a kind of memory of the pebble.

Right and below:
Stitched limpets. Small holes are drilled into limpet shells, allowing a round warp to be threaded into the hole in the middle of each shell. Needle weaving in and out builds up a woven surface within the shell frame.

I have worked a lot with limpet shells *(Patella vulgata)* with tiny holes drilled so that I can stitch through them. I work with the shells that already have a central hole in them, which makes it a lot easier to pass my needle backwards and forwards through the 'spokes' of the circular warp I create. This is a similar technique to that used in making 'Dorset buttons', where stitches cross the circle, like spokes in a wheel, and then the thread is woven around and around this little warp. Inside a limpet shell this is all done on a very small scale, and I use a needle to do the weaving. A plane is built up with thread as I weave around and around, until the whole of the shell inside – or much of its outside – is filled with that constructed surface.

Above: Stitched and woven chestnut shells. These were worked into after the chestnut shells had dried out.

Working with wood

Sticks, twigs and small pieces of driftwood can be wrapped with thread to make a simple warp for weaving into. Some of these would also be suitable for careful drilling into to enable a more stable warp structure. I have also woven into horse chestnut *(Aesculus hippocastanum)* shells that encased beautiful conkers, stitching through holes made with a pin, rather than a drill, once they've dried. This forms a 'warp'

Above: Stitched and woven chestnut shells. These were worked into when fresh, and then left to dry, distorting the woven surface.

for needle-weaving, either in a circular way as for the limpets on page 75, or with parallel stitches crossing the small void.

These wonderful little vessels are quite fleshy when they first drop from the tree, releasing their seed. As a result, they are easy to stitch through, but as they dry, they shrink considerably, distorting any stitches made while they are fresh. Allowing them to dry out first means that some don't retain such a deep vessel shape, but they are more stable.

Left: Driftwood with weave. Tiny warps are made by wrapping the wood, which can then be woven into.

Urban treasures

Some found objects may lend themselves to forming little frames that can be used to weave onto. An example of such an improvised frame is an old metal egg slicer, found at a bonfire site on agricultural land (shown right). All sorts of rubbish had been burnt on this site; what remained were the parts that were metal and therefore not combustible. This little metal frame was one of a whole series of objects that I collected from the site and worked with to create a number of responsive pieces.

I wrapped the object in the same way that I would wrap a wooden weaving frame and then wove a weft into my warp, filling up the space within the metal frame. Along with the other altered objects from the same site, this was then added to an oak-gall dye pot so that the tannins in the oak galls reacted with the metal of the object, together staining the constructed woven surface.

Left: Train ticket, stitched with needle weaving.

Above: *Lime Kiln Objects*. Woven egg slicer. Found metal object used as a frame for small-scale weaving.

Left: Woven match box. The sliding inside of a matchbox wrapped to form a warp with weave, incorporating spent matches.

Below: Woven cup lid. The plastic of this cup lid is easily pierced with a needle, allowing stitches to form a warp for small-scale weaving.

Other less robust materials might also lend themselves to forming a base for small-scale weave. Small boxes or other cardboard items (such as train tickets) can be stitched through or wound around to make a basic warp. Plastic items might also be stitched through or drilled to allow a warp to be formed. The cup lid and train ticket shown were worked on during a long train journey, on my way to teach a workshop on stitching with found objects. This is an example of seeing what materials are available at any one point in time and then working with what you have.

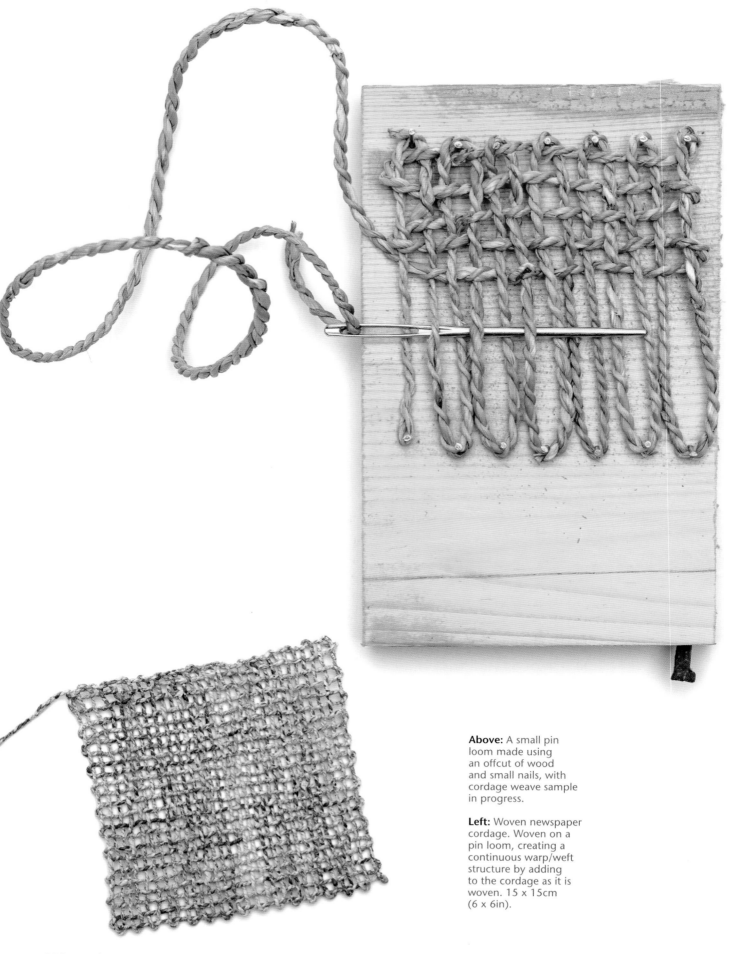

Above: A small pin loom made using an offcut of wood and small nails, with cordage weave sample in progress.

Left: Woven newspaper cordage. Woven on a pin loom, creating a continuous warp/weft structure by adding to the cordage as it is woven. 15 x 15cm (6 x 6in).

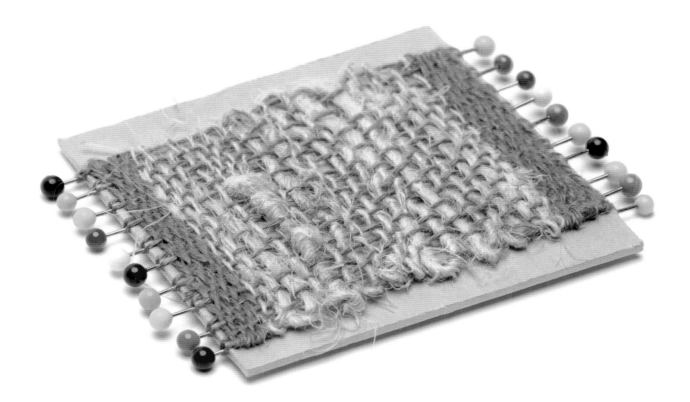

Improvised looms

What I've described on the previous page uses objects as frames for weaving and the woven surface remains permanently attached to the piece. Alternatively, there are a variety of ways for making improvised looms for creating a woven surface that is then removed from the frame once the structure is made. A basic way to form a small woven surface is to push pins into the end of thick card, wind a warp backwards and forwards around the pins and then weave into that. This will only work on a fairly small scale but means you can construct a woven surface with the bare minimum of equipment.

Simple pin looms can also be made by banging small nails into a piece of wood. A warp can then be wound onto the nails. It is possible to then weave into the warp using the same length of thread (or cordage), forming a structure with one continuous warp and weft. I often use this method to make samples with my plant-based cordage – this is how many of the small woven samples featured in this book were constructed. It allows me to make a structure with only that one material. A scaled-up version of this technique allows me to make larger woven structures with only one type of fibre and in one continuous thread structure.

Above: A small-scale pin loom made by pushing dressmaking pins into thick card and winding a warp around the pins.

Coiling

Coiling is another technique used in basketry to form flat surfaces or vessels. Coiling is a relatively quick way to build up a structure with a main core of material and a 'stitched' element that holds the coils together. A lovely example of coiling is seen in the construction of traditional bee 'skeps' (a traditional hive for keeping bees made of coiled straw or dried grass), using straw as the coiled material and split bramble for the stitching.

Some gathered materials may be less suitable for twisting into cordage and could lend themselves better to coiled structures and surfaces. When techniques or structures are new to me, I find it useful to experiment with a material that

Above: Bee skep, photographed at Heligan Gardens in Cornwall.

Below: Coiled vessel samples made with twisted newspaper and spun flax (linen) thread.

is readily available and may require less 'management' than some of the plant-based materials we've looked at so far.

Getting to grips with a technique at the same time as learning how to work with a particular material can be a step too far, and may result in frustration. Using something abundant and cheap like newspaper can be a good way of practising a structure first. When I teach cordage-making, I encourage students to use cloth or newspaper first, getting to know the basic technique before using plant material. This is just as applicable to coiling or wrapping.

A series of experiments with strips of newspaper and some paper string allowed me to practise coiling and try different ways of stitching the core element together. Once I was confident with the basic form, I could then use dampened plant material to make similar structures.

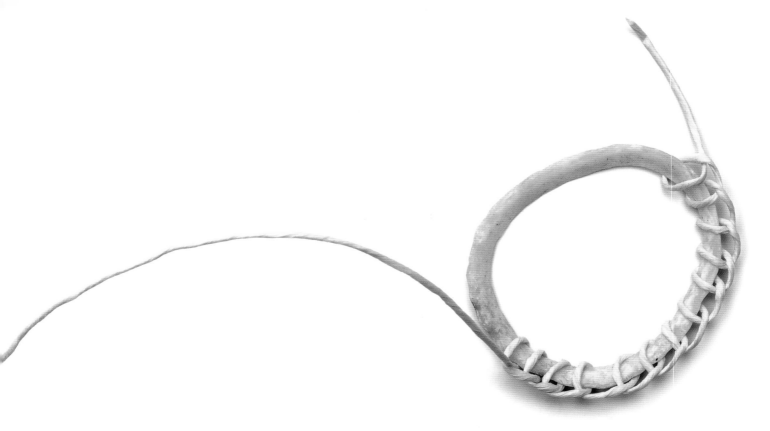

Looping

Above: Paper yarn looped onto a hoop, showing the start of a circular looped structure.

Below: Looped paper structures coated with mud and allowed to dry.

I started using looping as a way of exploring three-dimensional forms on a very small scale. Using a needle and thread, this is a version of detached buttonhole stitch. Working a buttonhole stitch around a ring or loop of thread and then continuing to build the stitches, increasing the number in each row in a circular motion, will result in an expanding surface. Using a thread with some inherent stiffness, such as a paper yarn, enables the build-up of something more structural and three-dimensional.

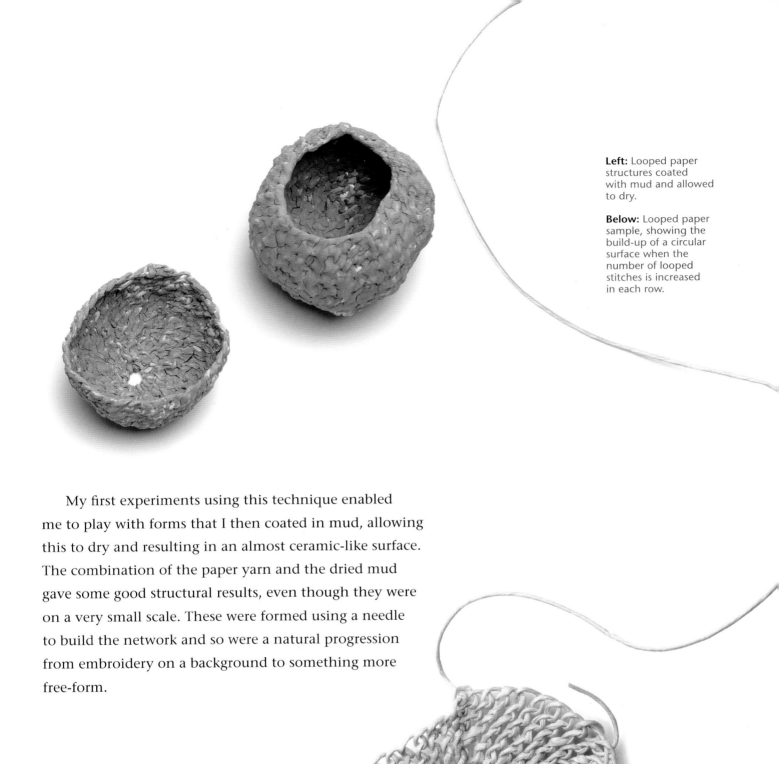

My first experiments using this technique enabled
me to play with forms that I then coated in mud, allowing
this to dry and resulting in an almost ceramic-like surface.
The combination of the paper yarn and the dried mud
gave some good structural results, even though they were
on a very small scale. These were formed using a needle
to build the network and so were a natural progression
from embroidery on a background to something more
free-form.

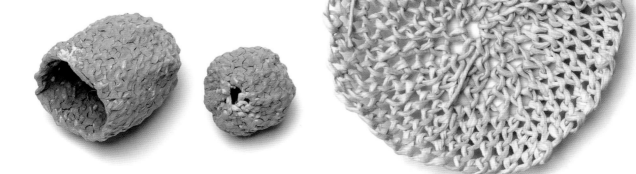

Using the same technique, but with softer linen thread and this time supported by working around found objects, I have worked over and around a series of different natural objects, including driftwood, small branches, shells and pebbles.

Looking to use more found materials rather than bought threads, I experimented with a range of beach-combed plastic ropes. Just as the nature and nuances of natural materials varies, these ropes differ hugely in their strength and properties, so it became an interesting exercise to get to know what each type was like to work with. Deconstructing the rope fibres to work with individual strands provided me with some useful material and an injection of bright colours that was very different from the natural and neutral tones of most of the materials I work with.

Above: Driftwood with looped linen thread and natural staining.

Below: Worn shell with paper yarn and found plastics stitched and wrapped.

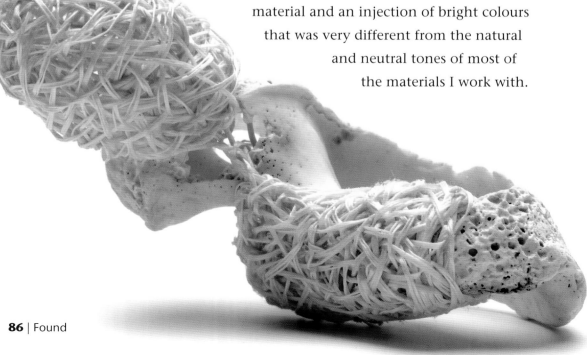

Above: Olive wood (some burnt) with looping in linen thread.

Right: Beachcombed bones with looping in plastics from deconstructed beach-combed ropes.

Nine Wrapped Stones

This group of objects, made for an exhibition, brings together a combination of some of the techniques we've looked at in this section. All the materials used here were gathered from my allotment, either found in the sheds, around the plot or grown, gathered and processed there. The nine stones were also from the plot, dug up when I was making a new path along one of the beds.

The stones gave me a starting point for scale and provided a form to work around. This was particularly important for some of the softer materials, which benefitted from the support of the stone to keep the constructed form.

Clockwise from back:
Looped newspaper
cordage with stone;
looped sweetcorn husk
cordage with stone;
hand-spun flax (linen)
twined onto soft rush
with stone.

Left: *Nine Wrapped
Stones*. Clockwise from
far left: plastic grid with
looped iris-leaf cordage
with stone; twined
dandelion stems
with stone; looped
daffodil-leaf cordage
with stone; braided
dandelion stems with
stone and stitching
in re-purposed found
plastic; looped bramble
fibre cordage with
stone; random
weave bindweed
stems with stone.

Bringing different materials together in this way is something I find satisfying.
I am intrigued by the mixture of found objects and grown fibres and I like the
fact that there are so many potential ways to bring them together: there are
endless possibilities for creating and responding to conversations between
the different materials.

Each of these objects stands alone and could be removed from the group
to tell its own story, but bringing them together, arranging them in different
ways and allowing them to remain in each other's company seems fitting.
They are of the same place, even though their constituent parts have diverse
starting points.

Above: Blackthorn 'pins'
through linen cloth.

Chapter 5

Gathered

Grass

Grass is the most widely accessible of plant materials. If it is worked fresh, then some shrinkage will occur as it dries. If it is gathered dry, or is allowed to dry out, then it should be dampened to work with, just like any other plant material.

Picking a handful of grass in whatever location you are in and twisting it into a cord is one of the most immediate ways you can respond creatively to the environment around you. This can also be a useful way of creating instant string for tying something up in the garden if you don't have any other twine to hand.

Once twisted into a cord or string, this can then be used to form a constructed surface or structure. When making a looped structure with cordage, it is best to twist a section up to 1m (3ft) in length, loop that into the structure and then add another section onto the length. This is because the looping requires the whole length to pass through the previous hole, which is different to constructing a knitted or crocheted structure (where you work off a ball of yarn and just a small part is passed through previous holes to construct the surface).

Right: *Walking Balls.* A series of balls made with various materials gathered whilst walking and used as a record of each place visited. Materials include different grasses (twisted into cordage), seaweed, moss and bracken.

Above: A piece of cordage quickly made with fresh grass.

Walking balls

Walking in different places and habitats means coming across different types of material that can be gathered and worked with to make creative responses or records of the location. A series of balls of material made in different places formed such a record for me. These objects, which were made sometimes quickly and sometimes slowly in each place, form a tangible link to their respective places. Each material required slightly different handling and I learnt about the physical properties of each as I worked with them.

This process of wrapping material found on location is an immediate way of responding to the material of that place and can be used for natural or synthetic materials. It can be done while on the move, literally making as you walk. Or material can be gathered and brought together while stationary but still made on location.

Common Agency Projects

Shane Waltener's site-specific sculptures and installations engage with the natural or built environment.

The process of making, using seasonal plant material, in projects that are often participatory and collaborative, facilitates the exchange of personal, social and cultural narratives, creating new knowledge and imaginaries.

During COVID-19 restrictions, Shane worked with dance artist Laura Glaser, meeting weekly in parks and commons. Public spaces developed a new function: more than safe spaces to socialize in, they became cultural centres where people went to be entertained and share ideas and experiences.

Working outdoors, the artists developed a number of performances, Commoning Actions #1–15, that address the idea of nature as commons. They were developed through movement improvisation and discussions between the artists, interested park-goers and invited collaborators. Inspired by the idea of the commons, the performances are creative collaborative actions affirming that we and all that is around us have equal agency.

While developing this work, Shane and Laura formed the artist collective Common Agency Projects (CAP) and wrote the following manifesto outlining their values, aims and methodology:

Here is CAP's recipe for 'Commoning Action #6: how to build inclusive and sustainable enclosures':

Materials:
- grass, 30cm (12in) tall or longer
- 1+ commoners

Score:
1. Locate a grassy area to perform the action in.

2. Proceed to plait grasses close to the ground as you would a French plait, adding more grass to the three strands you are plaiting as you go.

3. Do this at a regular working rhythm and make sure you are working towards a patch of ground providing you with sufficient grass to plait with. Change your course accordingly.

4. When your plait crosses another (yours or another commoner's), your action is complete.

5. Move away from the grassy enclosure(s) you have created knowing they will compost, adding nutrients to the soil, until the next season when the area will be open ground again.

Left and above: Common Agency Projects (artists Shane Waltener and Laura Glaser) performing 'Commoning Actions' on Wanstead Flats, London, 2020.

CAP's *working with* manifesto:
- working with nature as a commons.
- working with material and plant agency.
- working with the weather and the seasons.
- working with ephemerality, change and repetition.
- working with less, but better.
- working with movement and stillness.
- working with risk and simplicity.
- working with spontaneity in the here and now.
- working with site as a space for improvisation and performance.
- working with space and time and material as holders of memory and history.
- working with the whole body and all the senses.
- working with one another as part of everything around us.

Wild wool

Walking in areas of countryside where there is livestock means you might come across wool or hair caught on hedges, fences or walls. Cattle, horse or sheep will often rub against these boundaries. In the Shetland Isles, wool caught in this way is called 'henty leggits' or 'henty lags' and has a history of being gathered and used as part of the rich knitting tradition in that part of Scotland. Barbed wire fencing is good at catching these scraps of wool, and coming across an area where sheep have gathered and left tufts of it hanging from the fence like a row of flags can be quite beautiful. Even the smallest bundle of gathered wool can be spun or twisted to form a record of that place visited. These small balls were crudely spun from wool gathered on local walks and are another kind of 'walking ball'.

A friend and her late husband, as keen walkers, often gathered wool from their walks in Scotland and the Yorkshire Dales. They didn't go out intentionally to collect wool but were often moved to do so when they found it. When there was enough to make it worthwhile, they would share the tasks of carding, spinning and knitting the wool.

Left: Sheep's wool caught on fences where the animals rub or gather.

Above: Wool gathered on walks, spun and knitted by a friend.

Right: Collecting wool from fences whilst walking in the countryside.

Wild plastics

Plastic pollution has become a pressing issue for wildlife and the health of our seas, with recognition of the severity of the problem growing in recent years. Organisations such as 2 Minute Foundation have helped spread awareness and encourage small acts of responsibility that can help clean up coastal areas. However often beaches are cleaned, the persistence of plastics in the environment is a problem that is going to be around for a very long time. I was particularly aware of how such pollution travels when I visited parts of the Outer Hebrides, and found huge amounts of plastics washed up on the remote beaches.

Although picking up these plastics removes them from the beach or the sea, and perhaps means some can be recycled, this issue will only really be addressed by reducing the amount of plastics we use. Gathering as I walked, I felt that using these plastics as materials to make with is a suitable response as an artist to the depressing reality of their presence. As Julie Decker explains in *Gyre: The Plastic Ocean* (see Further Reading, page 124):

Below: *Walking Balls: Plastics.* A series of balls made with plastics found whilst walking in coastal locations.

Artists offer public insights that they hope will lead to a greater understanding, broader perspective, and celebration of our natural world ... This new environmental art is not passive or detached. It suggests activism, not observation; science, not romanticism; and new knowledge, not conventional wisdom.

Some of these gathered ropes initiated an immediate creative response by way of forming some of the walking balls that I mentioned earlier (see page 92). Others invited a more considered investigation, even dissection. By deconstructing the various ropes, I found I was able to understand the different types of plastic fibre better and start to explore ways in which I might use them.

Some of the softer fibres seemed initially more attractive to work with, feeling in the hand more like the natural fibres I am accustomed to working with. However, these were also weaker and tended to snap and fray. Some of the harder braided ropes, once separated down to their individual strands were surprisingly pleasing to work with; I found that I could make quite intricate structures that were self-supporting because of the wiry nature of the threads.

These investigations formed the basis of my work on *Galling*, a piece of work inspired by the structures that are formed by plants in response to the activity of gall wasps (see page 117).

Above and below:
Galling (2016). A series of pieces using beach-combed plastic objects and deconstructed ropes to form gall-like structures. Looping, wrapping and twining.

Glorious mud

I have already mentioned the way I used mud on looped paper yarn structures to create small experimental vessels (see page 85). The mud used in these pieces was particularly silky estuarine mud gathered while walking and with the intention of using it in the studio. By coating thread and paper with gathered mud, then allowing it to dry out, I found that I could make small sculptural forms that have a sense of place attached to them. Extending this idea into other surfaces led me to experiment with a series of small book forms that were coated in mud from different places that I visited, resulting in a series of 'walking books'.

Above and right:
Walking Books (2017). Paper, linen and mud. Handmade Coptic-bound books coated in mud from a variety of locations.

The colour of the mud varies significantly between places, but so does the texture, viscosity and the way that it dries on the surface it is applied to. Earth pigments are currently experiencing a surge in interest, as artists explore ways to make their practice and materials more in tune with nature. There are refined approaches to this, involving gathering and crushing rock and earth to use with natural binders to make different types of paint. Literally scooping up a handful of the earth beneath your feet and spreading it onto a surface is a more primitive approach but has the same essence of engagement with place and material.

Above: Knotted cube with mud (2016). Knotted cotton and mud. 5 x 5 x 5cm (2 x 2 x 2in).

Needles and pins

Using tools that are made from found and gathered materials can be particularly satisfying. Experimenting with found mark-making tools such as feathers, sticks and home-made brushes can result in some wonderfully expressive lines and marks. Extending this into tools for textile work could be equally meaningful. The collection of needles and hooks shown here are items from my own studio tool kit. Using a needle that you know is handmade and crafted from a found natural resource adds a layer of engagement with material that will enhance the process.

Blackthorn grows abundantly in the UK, making a common appearance in the hedgerows. The thorns can be long and strong, which makes hedgerow foraging a prickly activity, but these thorns can also be used as improvised pins and needles.

Other species with thorns of different dimensions could be used to pin textile elements together. Pruning my fruit bushes on the allotment each winter results in a pile of prickly gooseberry branches. These could just be composted along with other plant debris, but the spikes are fine and sharp and can be removed from the twigs with care and kept for use as natural pins.

Far left: Blackthorn (*Prunus spinosa*) branch with thorns still attached.

Above left: Thorns removed from a blackthorn branch, trimmed and dried for use as pins.

Below left: Wooden needles and crochet hooks, gifted or whittled from found twigs.

Right: Blackthorn 'pins' through linen cloth, most with bark still present. Lone pin peeled to reveal lighter wood.

Above: *Dandelion strip cloth
ii,* (2021). Dandelion stems
(*Taraxacum officinale*), gathered
after flowering, dried, braided
and stitched together with more
stems to form a flexible surface.
41 x 32cm (16 x 12½in)

Chapter 6

Re-purposed

Paper string

Each type of paper will have different characteristics, and some will lend themselves well to cordage-making. Others may be too stiff and not so easy to twist or roll cleanly. The best way to find out how paper feels in the fingers is to try twisting a bit. The width of the strips you use may also affect how easily a type of paper twists. Try cutting strips but also tearing against the edge of a ruler for a softer edge. Wetting paper before twisting, as you would do with plant fibres, is generally not going to work, as it may weaken it. I find that a damp sponge will wet my fingers just enough to help roll the paper, touching the sponge between every few twists, helping to make a firm and smooth string.

Above left: Cordage made from newspaper.

Above right: Cordage made from re-purposed tissue-paper packaging.

When paper does twist well into cordage it can make a surprisingly strong string and this can be used to make some robust structures. Newspaper is an ideal starting point as the paper is relatively soft and is easy to source. The ink will rub off on your fingers as you work, but this easily washes away.

If you are used to using a drop spindle or spinning wheel you could also spin strips of newspaper into a spun thread. This will just have twist in one direction but the stiffness of paper will tend to hold the twist in place. Two strands could be plied together to make a stronger or thicker yarn.

Left: *Newspaper Vessel* (2021). Looped cordage made from newspaper. 12 x 12 x 7cm (4¾ x 4¾ x 2¾in).

Paper boxes

Some papers that are crisp or stiff can be softened by scrunching, rolling and kneading in your hands. This softens the fibres and can shift the properties of the sheet to something much more cloth-like.

If a type of paper is too stiff for rolling into cordage then it may lend itself to other manipulation. I have experimented with various papers found in my allotment sheds, threading strips through other materials, folding small boxes and weaving strips of thicker card. Stitching through paper can be very satisfying. I find it is best to make holes first with a round-headed pin, then I can stitch through from both sides without having to guess where to bring my needle up from behind.

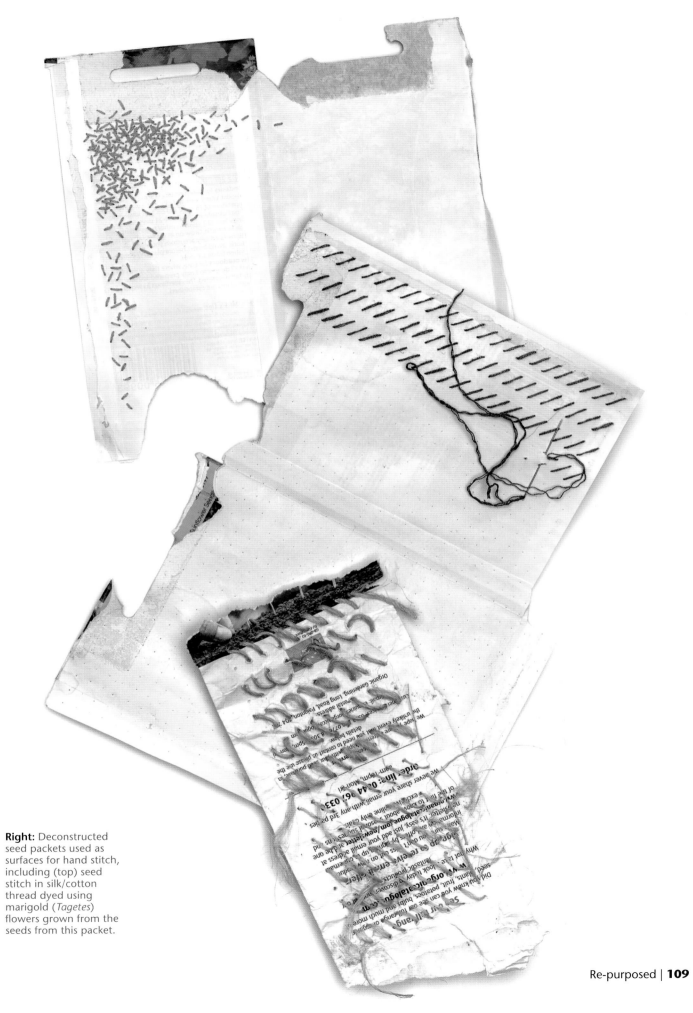

Right: Deconstructed seed packets used as surfaces for hand stitch, including (top) seed stitch in silk/cotton thread dyed using marigold (*Tagetes*) flowers grown from the seeds from this packet.

Re-purposed plastics

Using the same technique for rolling and twisting plant material or strips of paper, found plastics can also be made into cordage or string. Exploring the objects and materials that I inherited with my allotment plot saw me trying assorted types of plastic from plant pots that could be cut down into fine strips, plastic sacks, deconstructed plastic rope and bubble wrap.

The bubble wrap was a pleasant surprise. I hadn't expected it to be nice to work with, but its softness in the fingers meant it made a good string with strength and a silvery sparkle that contrasts with the matt nature of many of the other materials I work with. Some of the

Left: Experimental sample using found plastics from the allotment: cable tie with looped strips of plastic sacking.

Above right: Cordage made with re-purposed bubble wrap found in the allotment shed and looped onto a broken plant-pot shard.

Right: Cordage made from one whole supermarket carrier bag and looped plastic bag, made from one whole supermarket carrier bag.

stiffer plastics were not so easy to work with, but with a bit of perseverance, could be manipulated in interesting ways.

Considering the potential of a plastic carrier bag from a supermarket that had been re-used many times and was no longer reliable as a bag, I cut the bag into strips and twisted it into a length of cordage. One carrier bag made approximately 7m (23ft) of cordage. A second bag was treated similarly, but this time the cordage was formed for about 1m (3ft) then looped into a new smaller bag shape. Once that section was looped then the next length was formed, then looped and so on, until the whole bag had been re-formed as a new, much smaller kind of bag.

Renewed cloth

Part of my investigations into the materials available on my allotment plot led to cordage-making with some of the rags found there. My guess is that these cotton cloths were originally curtains or other household fabrics, which had already been repurposed as cloths for wiping and drying tools and surfaces on the allotment plot by previous owners.

The cloths that were found in the shed were still relatively strong. Those that had been left outside, probably for months or years previously, were weathered and weakened by the elements. Tearing these cloths down into strips to make cordage with immediately demonstrated this difference in the structural integrity of the fibres. The ones from outside tore much more easily and were fragile. Even the texture of these otherwise similar fabrics felt different in my hands as I twisted them into string.

A commission by the clothing company Toast and Kettles Yard Gallery, Cambridge, came my way as part of a project to encourage people to think about the longevity of their clothing and how cloth can be mended, re-purposed and renewed. I was sent a box of fabrics – offcuts, samples, leftover pieces from the commercial making of clothes – and invited to work creatively with them, re-purposing them into something 'unique and unexpected'.

Through mindful handling of the material, observing and examining, I learnt about the properties and possibilities that each piece of fabric presented. Stripping the cloth down and twisting by hand, I became aware of the subtle differences between each fibre and cloth construction type. Surface pattern was abstracted with the rhythm of twisted strands, and the resulting 36 balls of re-worked threads became a collection that could be arranged tonally.

Above left: Ball of cordage made with cloth found in the allotment shed.

Above right: Looped cloth cordage vessel. Made with waste cloth from Toast, part of sampling for the (re)new project.

Right: (re)new threads: 36 balls of hand-twisted cordage made using waste fabrics.

Reworked objects

Some of the objects I find serve as a source of study and inspiration. Other items I find ways to work with by adding constructed elements from different materials. I've already shown examples of items that I've made holes in, through which I can thread, stitch or weave. Some materials are easier to make holes in than others, either by pushing a sharp pin through or by clamping the object and drilling holes through. For some materials I must get help with drilling.

A set of old tools found in my allotment sheds are an example. I knew I wanted to make holes in them through which I could thread my cordage, but this required some slightly specialized tools. The loan of a particular type of drill from a friend (along with a tutorial in how to safely use it) enabled me to drill the holes I wanted in the various metal

Above: *Hybrid 5: Pink Trowel* (2021). Random weave bindweed stems with found tool.
22 x 7 x 6cm
(8½ x 2¾ x 2½in)

Above: *Hybrid 2: Trowel* (2020). Looped daffodil leaf cordage with found tool. 32 x 8 x 5cm (12½ x 3¼ x 2in).

Below: *Hybrid 6: Fork* (2021). Looped nettle fibre cordage with found tool. 28 x 25 x 3cm (11 x 10 x 1¼in).

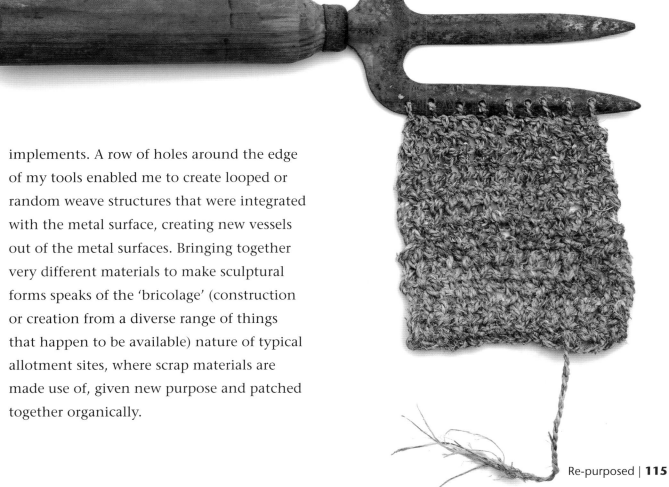

implements. A row of holes around the edge of my tools enabled me to create looped or random weave structures that were integrated with the metal surface, creating new vessels out of the metal surfaces. Bringing together very different materials to make sculptural forms speaks of the 'bricolage' (construction or creation from a diverse range of things that happen to be available) nature of typical allotment sites, where scrap materials are made use of, given new purpose and patched together organically.

Offcuts

When working with materials that are hard won or limited in supply, I find that even the smallest scraps and offcuts can become important. It is difficult to discard these leftovers once you notice and start to appreciate their value. I often keep these tiny snippets, allowing them to accumulate and collect them together in paper boxes, curating them on my studio desk. Sometimes they eventually find their way into the compost bin, but only after I've considered and contemplated their use.

Playing about with these small pieces can lead to interesting developments, noticing the detail in the ever-decreasing units and looking for ways to work with them. A set of nettle stems that were left over after I had stripped off the useable fibre were explored in this way. Exploring ways of joining them led me to thread them together, making new units that could be experimented with further. Not yet (and maybe never) resolved more than this, they remain on my studio desk, waiting to see where they might lead me.

Above: Origami paper boxes with dandelion- and nettle-stem offcuts, left over after trimming cordage and braiding works.

Formed objects

Some found objects and materials are too fragile or fleeting to be made use of physically. They can of course be studied, photographed, drawn, described and remembered. Records made in these various ways can then inform the surfaces and structures that we develop, either as a direct and obvious influence or as part of a general understanding of surface and form.

Sketching and drawing found objects is a useful way of getting to know them, understanding their detail and exploring their properties. I find that making a series of visual studies, either as loose and quick or as slow detailed drawings, helps provide a way into knowing the item and unlocking the inspiration that might come from it.

Above: Sketchbook drawings of plant galls, used to inform 3D sampling for *Galling*.

Below: Paper samples for *Galling* (left) and (right) beachcombed toothbrush with paper and found plastics wrapped and stitched, part of *Galling* (2016).

A series of drawn sketches and then quick three-dimensional experiments using paper, which could also be thought of as sketches, was my starting point for developing *Galling* (shown right). These 2D and 3D sketches were of as many different types of gall as I could find. Galls are swellings or structures on the surfaces of plants that are formed in response to parasitic insects. I collect oak galls for making ink with, but there are galls that form on lots of different plant species, and I became interested in the way that the plant creates a structure as a response to the disruption of the insect.

The series started by making small 'growths' to attach to found natural objects (a stick and a bone) and initially appeared as if they might be naturally formed galls, then moved onto more gaudy plastic objects. This embodied a fanciful suggestion that insects might eventually evolve to make use of the plastics persisting in our environment.

Above: Sketchbook drawing of a bird's nest. Pencil and charcoal.

Vessels and nests

I am increasingly drawn to vessel forms and find I use them more and more in my work, many examples of which are included in this book. I've always loved bowls, baskets and pots. A hollow container that might have function, but also can contain, enclose and protect other items, has a universal appeal. Even an empty vessel holds space and frames it, suggesting potential.

Natural vessels are an obvious starting point for visual research. Seed cases, shells and nests can be found, collected and studied, giving information and understanding about endlessly varied structures and properties.

- How deep or shallow is the concave form?
- Are the vessel walls solid or are there gaps?
- Is the vessel fragile or strong?
- Does the surface texture vary between the outside and inside of the form?
- Is the form made up of different materials or structural elements?

Above: *Ticket Nest* (2021). Vessel formed from re-purposed train tickets, cut into long strips for random weave. 15 x 15 x 8cm (6 x 6 x 3¼in).

Studying these properties, giving time to understand the form visually by making notes and really getting to know the detail that is present, will mean that any work made in response to it will be better informed and more nuanced as a result.

Apple vessels

Drawings of bird-pecked fruit on the autumnal allotment helped inform my *Apple Vessels*. My sketches were done in homemade ink, giving another layer of connection to the place where the apples were grown and sculpted by the birds on the plot. Drawing the detail of these ephemeral objects was important as they rot away quickly. I then started making my vessels using looped paper yarn formed around whole apples.

Once they were formed, I dyed the vessels with applewood ink I had made from pruned branches of the same apple trees. Some of the vessels enclosed the apple fully; others just came part way around the apple. In each case, the apple was allowed to dry and shrink within the form, leaving the shell of the apple shape just like the ephemeral vessels that the birds left behind.

Left: Sketchbook drawing of bird-pecked apples from the allotment. Pencil with home-made botanical ink.

Below: *Apple Vessels* (2019). Looped paper yarn, ink made from apple wood and iron with dried apples. Various dimensions up to 8cm (3¼in).

Final Thoughts

In writing this book, I set out with the aim of sharing my ongoing experience of using grown and gathered materials in my work, in the hope that this might enable others to explore similar adjustments in their practice. I feel passionately that we can (and should) take responsibility for our own actions. By embracing methods and approaches that are sustainable and mindful, we can help shift our collective relationship to nature. There is so much richness to be found all around us, every day.

With the COVID-19 pandemic, we were all forced to stay closer to home. For many this led to a rediscovery of the wonder and value that can be found if we slow down, take notice and care for our immediate place in the world. Many of the processes that I have described here take time to undertake and to understand. I am still learning and hope that will always be the case. That slow learning and appreciation for the cycles of the natural world brings with it a richness of experience, and is surely worth taking time to develop.

Left: *Dandelion Strip Cloth ii* (2021). Dandelion stems, gathered after flowering, dried, braided and stitched together with more stems to form a flexible surface. 41 x 32cm (16¼ x 12½in)

Further Reading

Baines, P. (1989) *Linen. Hand spinning and weaving.* Batsford, London

Barber, E. W. (1994) *Women's Work: The First 20,000 Years – Women, Cloth and Society in Early Times.* Norton, New York.

Bunn, S. & Mitchell, V. (eds) (2021) *The Material Culture of Basketry: Practice, Skill and Embodied Knowledge.* Bloomsbury Visual Arts, London.

Burgess, R. (2019) *Fibershed: Growing a Movement of Farmers, Fashion Activists and Makers for a New Textile Economy.* Chelsea Green Publishing, Vermont.

Chinery, M. (2011) *Britain's Plant Galls: A Photographic Guide.* Wild Guides, Hampshire.

Crouch, D. (2003) *The Art of Allotments: Culture and Cultivation.* Five Leaves, Nottingham.

Decker, J. (2014) *Gyre: The Plastic Ocean.* Booth-Clibborn Editions, London.

Edom, G. (2019) *From Sting to Spin – A History of Nettle Fibre.* Urtica Books, Bognor Regis.

Flintoff, J-P. (2010) *Sew Your Own.* Profile Books, London.

Ford, B. (2017) *Yarn from Wild Nettles: A Practical Guide.* Birte Ford.

Fox, A. (2015) *Natural Processes in Textile Art.* Batsford, London.

Fox, A. (2016) *Findings.* Stitch:Print:Weave Press, Bradford

Fox, A (2020) *Plot 105.* Stitch:Print:Weave Press, Bradford

Gaustad, S. (2014) *The Practical Spinner's Guide: Cotton, Flax, Hemp.* Interweave, Loveland.

Harding, S. & Waltener, S. (2012) *Practical Basketry Techniques.* A & C Black Publishers, London.

Hurcombe, L. (2014) *Perishable Material Culture in Prehistory: Investigating the Missing Majority.* Routledge, Abingdon.

Kimmerer, R. W. (2020) *Braiding Sweetgrass: Indigenous Wisdom, Scientific Knowledge and the Teachings of Plants.* Penguin, London.

Mabey, R. (2010) *Weeds: How Vagabond Plants Gatecrashed Civilisation and Changed the Way We Think About Nature.* Profile Books, London.

Miller in: Adamson, G. & Kelley, V. Eds. (2013) *Surface Tensions: Surface, Finish and the Meaning of Objects.* Manchester: Manchester University Press.

Ogilvy, S (2021) *Nests.* Particular Books, London.

Textile Study Group (2017) *DIS/rupt.* Stitch:Print:Weave Press, Bradford.

Textile Study Group (2020) *Insights.* Textile Study Group, Bradford.

Walpole, L. (1989) *Creative Basket Making.* North Light Books, Cincinnati.

Walpole, L. (1989) *Crafty Containers From Recycled Materials.* Search Press, Kent.

Warren, P. (2006) *101 Uses for Stinging Nettles.* Wildeye, Norfolk.

Zawinski, D. (2015) *In the Footsteps of Sheep.* Schoolhouse Press, Pittsville.

Resources

The 2 Minute Foundation
beachclean.net, #2minutebeachclean
A registered charity devoted to cleaning up the planet
2 minutes at a time.

Chrysalis Arts Department
chrysalisarts.com/resources/greening-arts-practice-guide
A guide for artists wanting to develop environmentally
responsible practice.

Common Ground
commonground.org.uk
A charity at the forefront of conservation and
environmental education in England.

We Are Commoners
craftspace.co.uk/wearecommoners/
Artists, exhibitions and other acts of commoning.

Fibershed
Fibershed.org
A community of fibre and dye growers, processors,
makers and manufacturers.

Flaxland
Flaxland.co.uk
Information on growing and processing flax.

R-Space Gallery
linenbiennalenorthernireland.com
A cultural celebration of Lisburn's linen history.

Nettles for Textiles
nettlesfortextiles.org.uk
All about nettles, plus information about
Allan Brown's nettle cloth

The Linen Project
thelinenproject.online

Contributors

Allan Brown
@hedgerow.couture

Hillary Waters Fayle
www.hillarywfayle.com

Laura Glaser
www.lauraglaser.com

Penny Maltby
@ministryofstraw
www.pennymaltby.co.uk

Shane Waltener
www.shanewaltener.com

Index

Illustrations are in **bold**.

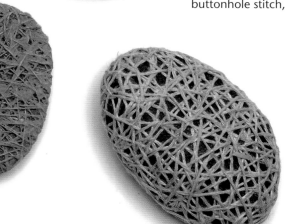

Acknowledgements

Above: Gathering plastics on the beach, South Uist, Outer Hebrides.

I would like to thank the following:

Susie Gillespie for sharing her experience with growing, processing and spinning flax. The members of the Textile Study Group for peer support, mentoring and friendship. My allotment neighbours for the shared love of our little corner of West Yorkshire and what grows there. Jonathan Fox for reading and help with those allotment jobs that are too big for one. Tina Persaud and Kristy Richardson at Batsford for supporting and producing this book. Michael Wicks for photographing my work so beautifully. My network of supporters, readers and students – this is for you.

Image credits

All photographs by Michael Wicks except for the following: P7, p9 (allotment shed), p11, p14, p16, p17, p22, p23, p24, p26, p31, p46 (Oak Leaf Quilt), p56, p66 (leaf stems on pavement), p72 (stop stone), p82 (bee skep), p96, p97 (gathering wool), p128 by Alice Fox. P9 (Hybrid Objects), p33, p57 (scraping fibre) by Sarah Mason. P37 by Allan Brown. P50 by David Hunter Hale. P51 by Hillary Waters Fayle. P52 by Annette Wilson. P64, p65 by Penny Maltby. P94 by Laura Glaser. P95 by Felicity Crawshaw.